S 250

# EVERYTHING IS POSSIBLE

Our Sudan Years

# EVERYTHING IS POSSIBLE
## Our Sudan Years

Margaret & Alick Potter

ALAN SUTTON
1984

Alan Sutton Publishing Limited
Brunswick Road · Gloucester

First published 1984

Copyright © 1984 Margaret & Alick Potter

All rights reserved. No part of this publication may be reproduced, stored in a retrieval system, or transmitted, in any form or by any means, electronic, mechanical photocopying, recording or otherwise, without the prior permission of the publishers and copyright holder.

**British Library Cataloguing in Publication Data**

Potter, Margaret
1. Sudan—Social life and customs
I. Title   II. Potter, Alick
962.4′04    DT131

ISBN 0-86299-125-0

The drawing on the half-title shows the top of the Mahdi's tomb in Omdurman – all that survived its desecration by Kitchener.

The calligraphic motif on the title page is a stylised version by Osman Waqialla of the Arabic 'Kullu mumkin', which can be translated 'Everything is possible'. In Arabic-speaking Sudan any call for help almost invariably drew the reply, 'Kullu mumkin' – accompanied by smiles or laughter. So often heard and so deeply imprinted on our memories, this phrase seems an appropriate title for a book devoted largely to people of the Sudan.

Typesetting and origination by
Alan Sutton Publishing Limited
Photoset Erhardt 11/13
Printed in Great Britain

# Contents

|    |                                                              | page |
|----|--------------------------------------------------------------|------|
|    | Foreword                                                     | 7    |
|    | Maps                                                         | 10   |
|    | Prelude                                                      | 13   |
| 1  | Hassan Atabani's Touch                                       | 17   |
| 2  | Specialisms of the Sudan                                     | 27   |
| 3  | Roots                                                        | 35   |
| 4  | The Finger of Allah<br>*Act One* – Hall of Success           | 39   |
| 5  | The Finger of Allah<br>*Act Two* – El Hamdulillah            | 53   |
| 6  | The Finger of Allah<br>*Act Three* – An Old Woman dressed in Black Rags | 61   |
| 7  | Travellers in an Antique Land                                | 73   |
| 8  | Aeroplanes are not yet among Stocked Items                   | 85   |
| 9  | Brotherhood of Man                                           | 93   |
| 10 | Blow, bugle, blow . . .                                      | 101  |
| 11 | Going Underground                                            | 111  |
| 12 | U.F.O.                                                       | 117  |
| 13 | Tell me, Grandfather                                         | 129  |
| 14 | Suakin Besieged                                              | 147  |
| 15 | Nubie                                                        | 157  |
| 16 | The Resident Engineer & The Huq                              | 163  |
| 17 | Dr Wenzel takes the biscuit                                  | 169  |
| 18 | Place of Birth: Heathrow                                     | 179  |
|    | Acknowledgements                                             | 187  |
|    | A Note about Books                                           | 188  |
|    | Index                                                        | 189  |

# Foreword

Returning from Europe after summer leave and descending from the plane at Wadi Halfa, travellers were hit by an astounding heat, a dry intense heat under which outlines, whether of rocks and stones or buildings, were lost in a shimmering haze. The river Nile, its banks dark with palm trees or the lively green of cultivations, flowed peacefully through desert sands which burnt one's feet through the soles of shoes. The travellers must either return to the plane to fly on to somewhat cooler Khartoum, or take the train from Wadi Halfa for a 27-hour journey to the same destination. Another year's work was about to begin.

Following the drama of the River War, in 1899 the Sudan became a Condominium under the joint rule of Egypt and Britain, until it achieved independence in 1956. For almost 60 years many British people lived and worked there, forming the Sudan Political Service, the Civil Service and the legal and medical services, and they also staffed the College which was to become the University of Khartoum. There were no foreign settlers – the land belonged to the people through the Government – and consequently all foreigners were transient though they might spend twenty-five years or more in the country. Apart from British, there were nationals of many countries bordering the Mediterranean – Greeks, Egyptians, Turks, Lebanese, Cypriots, Armenians and Italians – the majority of them merchants and business men, some professional men such as lawyers and doctors. Amongst the British (for whom I can speak), many became devoted to the country and to the Sudanese. All those on Government appointments were encouraged to learn the language of the area where they worked – Arabic in the northern and central Sudan, and a variety of indigenous languages in the south and west – and those in the Political Service, the Province Governors and District Commissioners, had to pass examinations in the appropriate language if they were to achieve promotion. As a result they came to know the people in their areas, to understand their way of life and customs, and many found great pleasure and satisfaction in their work. Those whose speciality took them out of

* Wall painting revealed during archaeological excavations at Debeira West.

Khartoum and into the countryside enjoyed the undoubted benefits of seeing the varied landscapes and meeting the country people in the markets, sometimes on camel treks, or on donkeys laden with fodder, visiting cultivations along the river banks, occasionally putting up for the night with local dignitaries, and having a taste of the lonely immensity of desert or the less awesome wooded lands and savanna further to the south.

Those who were largely confined to Khartoum were often professional men, economists and statisticians, teachers, solicitors, administrators of rail and airways, and many in the medical service. Khartoum was an artificial city consisting of Government offices and housing for its officials, shops and headquarters of multinational firms. It was well sprinkled with green from the gardens and shade trees planted along the roadsides. Few Sudanese lived there and the daily exodus for Omdurman at the end of the day's work at 2 p.m. led to a noisy scramble of cars and taxis, buses and clanking trams on the road to Omdurman bridge. Khartoum was a city of foreigners, all nationalities having clubs or centres of their own, and rarely did they mix, although after the Second World War less rigid attitudes increasingly gained a hold.

Throughout all this time, as might be expected, Sudanese national feeling grew, political parties made their presence felt, and by the early 1950's it was clear that the Sudan must shortly become independent from foreign rulers. Change was in the air, and even in the countryside the usual warmth of welcome could change to a cooler politeness.

On 1 January 1956, Independence was celebrated, and the Sudanese formed a Government and manned the entire administration of the country. There had been an effort by the British administration to train Sudanese for posts in the higher echelons of government service and some were in such posts, while for many years past the day-to-day work in the Government Departments had been in the hands of Sudanese officials. There were numerous Sudanese graduates of Khartoum University and some had further training abroad, returning with degrees or diplomas from universities overseas. In the great majority of cases a Sudanese official was found who was competent to take over the higher posts previously held by British (all of whom had to leave the country during 1955) and in the few cases where this was not so, foreign nationals of countries other than Britain were appointed for short interim periods. In the University, Sudanese staff had worked along with British teachers for some years, and the language of teaching, except for intrinsically Muslim subjects such as religion and Sharia law, was English, and this continued to be so.

It would not be true to suggest that the British administrators left the Sudan without some misgivings, particularly as they felt that there had been too short a time in the end to prepare adequately those who were taking on great responsibilities. However, the Sudanese were understandably determined, maintaining that it was their country and they wanted to take charge of it, even if initially they might make some mistakes. In fact, it seemed to run very well, though governments changed from time to time. By the time Margaret and Alick Potter arrived in Khartoum in August

1957 the initial euphoria associated with Independence had to some extent waned, and there was evidently an atmosphere of confidence and progress.

Readers of *Everything is Possible* will discover how greatly the Potters enjoyed their time in the Sudan, how much they learnt about it, how kind, informative and helpful their Sudanese colleagues were to them and how determined they were to travel as much as teaching commitments would allow and take in Sudan sights and sounds. It was a very special time for them. As Professor of Architecture (a new department in the University of Khartoum at that time), Alick was intent on studying local building methods and styles – ancient and modern – and did so with great energy and initiative. The examination hall, which he designed in collaboration with Ezra Levin, is witness to his inspiration – an elegant building constructed almost entirely of burnt mud bricks and Sudanese mahogany, its pointed roof seeming to lift it from the ground, its white internal walls enriched with giant calligraphy. It was seen as a triumph in the University. Margaret, his wife, is an artist and her affection for the Sudan and its people is evident in her delicate drawings – in the subjects she has intuitively chosen as much as in her talented work. Their warmth and hospitality, their interest and natural enjoyment of the country has led to lasting friendships with their Sudanese colleagues and former pupils who still call on them in their house in Wales.

Today the Sudan has fallen on harder times of the kind by which many developing countries are beset – economic problems leading to slow growth, hampered by shortage of oil and other essential raw materials, and with disaffection between north and south – a long running, warlike dispute which, temporarily settled in the 1970's with undertakings given by President Nimeiri, has again broken its bounds because of deep dissatisfaction in the south. In addition, thousands of refugees from troubled neighbouring countries have settled within the Sudan's ever-hospitable borders requiring the sort of care, medical attention and aids for living which, even at a minimal level, cannot really be afforded. Optimistic schemes for sugar and other agricultural produce proceed at a snail's pace, presumably for lack of funds – small boys in Khartoum market sell the bags meant for the Kenana sugar project for shopping bags, because there is still insufficient sugar with which to fill them.

Very few foreigners have written of their lives in the Sudan and *Everything is Possible* or *Kullu Mumkin* helps toward filling the gap. The book must be of considerable interest and enjoyment to readers who do not know the Sudan, and will certainly promote feelings of nostalgia and reminiscences of past travels in those who have lived there.

MARGARET SHINNIE
*(Archaeologist in the Sudan,*
*1946 onwards; assistant editor of*
The Geographical Journal *of the*
*Royal Geographical Society)*

**SUDAN'S NEIGHBOURS**

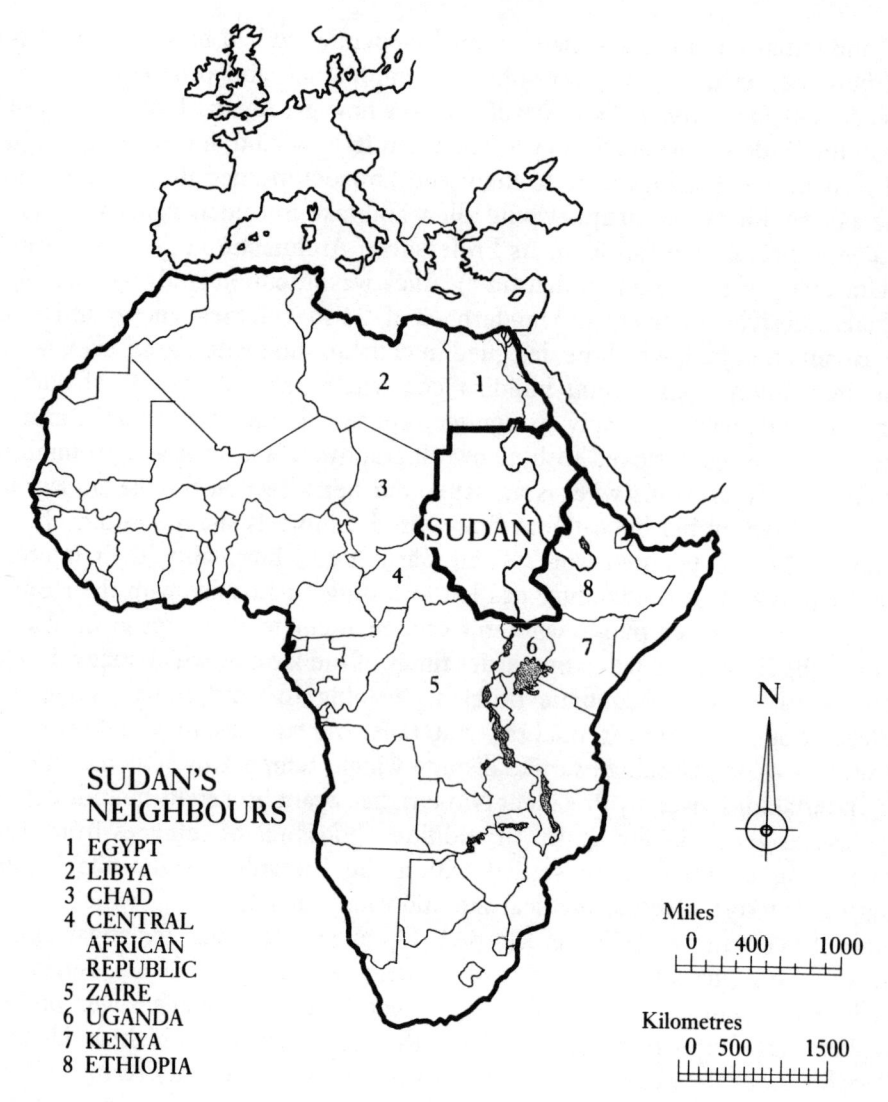

1 EGYPT
2 LIBYA
3 CHAD
4 CENTRAL AFRICAN REPUBLIC
5 ZAIRE
6 UGANDA
7 KENYA
8 ETHIOPIA

The area of the Sudan, over 2.5 million sq. km, is greater than that of Western Europe (excluding Scandinavia) and more than twice the area of all Scandinavian countries put together.

The Sudan is at present suffering economic hardship, in large measure due to a decline in its cotton exporting trade and an absence – or under-development – of its own raw materials. Despite this the Sudan continues to operate an open-door policy for refugees from neighbouring countries – some 700,000 in 1984, mainly from Ethiopia and Uganda.

*Names of states are shown as existing in 1984. The railway system is that of the period described in the book; since then it has been extended and some trunk roads built.*

*Maps*

*Everything is Possible*

*Humber and Railway Docks viewed from the Potters' living room*

## *Prelude*

Building, it seems, is part of nationhood. When a new nation comes into being, its historians are apt to refer to its creators as 'builders', and its leaders as 'architects'. Once independence is achieved, to be able to build is – as any postage stamp collector will vouch – one of the insignia of freedom, no less less vital an element in national self-esteem than the possession of armed forces or one's own international airline. And the justifiable pride in building is all the more intense if a nation happens to have a local vernacular – and, best of all, local materials – that can be used and developed.

Such might have been the undercurrent of Alick Potter's thinking when, rather to his surprise, he found himself appointed in the mid-1950s as the first professor of architecture in the Sudan, charged with the task of setting up a school of architecture in Khartoum university. And any such thoughts of his would have been echoed by his wife Margaret – for their friends insist that the two think almost as one. But in fact there was no time to construct a theoretical justification for what was largely a leap in the dark: events shot towards them and past them, dissolving into a blur like the tarmac that, soon, they would see swallowed up under the plane's wing.

On a hot Saturday afternoon in August, 1957, Alick Potter gave a lecture to Hull's local Georgian Society on some aspect of Italian Renaissance architecture. The two dashed home to pick up rucksacks, pre-packed with last-minute essentials; to lock the door finally on the view of Humber Dock that had delighted them for the last eight years; to read for the last time the faded legend, 'Plain Fare for Plain Folk' on the wall of Sam's Eating House next door; and by way of unforgettable East Anglian place-names like Omardyke Signal Box and Gilberdyke Junction, to arrive at length at a collection of hutments lurking behind mud-spattered hedges – Heathrow. That was a word of magic in Margaret's mind (as the last chapter of this book explains), capable of calling forth a vision of cherry blossom, Tudor brick and oak, the bustle of a farmyard. But the thoughts now were only of immediate realities – of the stewardess behind bearing the fragile leaving present of 'The Prospect of Hull', and of Africa ahead, beckoning . . .

Africa, the word, became flesh at Benghazi: a bumpy landing lit by madly flickering paraffin flares, a rush of sweet, hot smells invading the aircraft as soon as the door was rolled back. Then on, endlessly through blackness, until a random mass of lights revealed Omdurman and, moments later, a geometrical pattern of pinpricks outlined Kitchener's grid-iron plan for Khartoum. Into the pinkish glow that now announced dawn, the pair emerged, to be greeted by a chauffeur in pure white uniform who ushered them into his limousine.

Hull seemed aeons away. Was there anything at all that had happened there in the previous eight years of teaching, or at Liverpool before that, that could be of any conceivable relevance here, in this newly-independent country which until the previous year – and for 60 years before that – had been in fact if not in name under British rule? Many times the sun rose and set on that question, before it laid itself to rest. The students in the university who had been studying general science as the prelude to choosing between Engineering and Medicine were now free to make a third choice – Architecture. But in the Sudan at that time there was no academically based tradition of architecture: there was not even a word in the language to distinguish an architect from a *muhendis* or engineer. No wonder that, once the choices had been made, no more than four students were found in Alick Potter's new department.

This book does not set out to tell how, despite such a modest beginning, in the next seven or eight years a flourishing school of architecture became established in the Sudan which later developed into one of the main centres of architectural education in the Islamic world. Something of that theme may perhaps appear 'between the lines'. But the essence of these stories concerns learning rather than teaching: they tell how the Potters discovered riches in the Sudan, in its life and customs, in its traditions and historic remains, and above all in its human contacts.

*The South-East Prospect of Kingston upon Hull by Saml. & Nathl. Buck. 1745*

*The Pink Palace: Potters' first Khartoum home*

*Inside a country mosque*

# 1 Hassan Atabani's Touch

We first met Hassan a couple of days after our arrival in Africa. At that time he was chief architect of the Sudan Republic's Ministry of Public Building and Works. Although my position as a teacher of architecture at the University was independent of his Department, I think he felt we might need a friendly hand. No sooner had we been introduced than he said, in a way that left no doubt that he really meant it, how happy he would be if we would accompany him that same afternoon to Omdurman, which lies some two miles north of Khartoum.

Omdurman was – and still is – a marvellous shopping place. Almost everything on sale there is home-made or home-grown. Tinsmiths offer water dispensers* fashioned from discarded tin cans and trays with impressed arabesque designs; furniture makers turn bed and chair legs on lathes powered by strings attached to big toes; silversmiths bend wires for the enrichment of filigree boxes and goldsmiths hammer their metal into bead shapes indistinguishable from many found in ancient Nilotic tombs. There is endless variety, too, in the foodstuffs – and especially the fruits such as lemoon (limes), grapefruit, paw-paw and mango. This is because each small-holding farmer brings his own crops to market on panniers suspended from the saddle of his donkey, setting them out on the small piece of sandy earth which is all that he – or most of the other traders of Omdurman – has in the way of a shop.

Like a conjuror progressing from one trick to another, Hassan piloted us through the market quarter, waving his arms, keeping up an excited commentary, ever on the alert to spot the next item of special interest. He loved people, and often stopped to chat and chuckle. True to his initials, H. M. el Atabani's shopping was something of a royal progress!

---

* Water dispenser made from discarded tin cans

And then we came to an old lady selling beads. Her 'shop' was no different from the many others offering beads, which were of almost every conceivable kind: yellow, golden or chocolate-brown amber; or polished stones and pebbles, sometimes threaded on scraps of string or cloth tape; or turned wood; or glass – sometimes even, the parti-coloured glass used by nineteenth century traders. On the earth before her lay a flat circular tray of straw and a 'guffa', a flexible basket made of palm leaves. The old lady's stock was small: a few sweets, dried sunflower seeds – and four large, opaque beads of remarkably intense blue.

'You like them?' inquired Hassan, noting how Margaret's eyes were fixed on the ornaments.

'They're charming; completely beautiful,' she answered, unaware of the offer implied in his question. Nor did she observe Hassan bargaining and buying, until the beads were whipped away and wrapped in a fragment of old newspaper.

'Here,' said Hassan 'is your Welcome to Omdurman Present.' And her protestations were dismissed with unanswerable finality: 'Glass! Just nothing at all!'

Some people have the 'knack' of doing the right thing at the right moment. Instinctively they fish out an appropriate sum when the taxi reaches its destination. And when they give a present, it bears a stamp individual to the recipient, leaving no legacy of discomfort through either its lavishness or its triviality. Undoubtedly Hassan belonged to that happy band of those who have the 'knack' of giving. But 'knack' was not one of his words: as in due course we learned, he would himself have said that he had 'Just a Touch.'

As we climbed into Hassan's car, he said 'You wear the beads to ward off evil spirits. Blue alone is the colour which possesses this magical property.'

I doubt if he believed in this 'magical property' business. But minutes later, as we made a hair-raising journey home across the White Nile bridge, wobbling in top gear amidst donkeys and ancient clanging tram-cars and scoring innumerable near-misses with taxis, I had reason to be far less sure. For the colour of the car bonnet which preceded us safely through the chaos was blue – a particularly intense blue.

'Did you notice?' I asked Margaret later '... What do you think?'

'I think,' she replied firmly, 'that Africa is getting under your skin.'

Almost exactly twelve months later, I was visiting Hassan at the Ministry of Public Building and Works. His office occupied one corner of an inner quadrangle of the beautiful building which the Royal Engineers had constructed in the early days of the present century, next door to the Governor's Palace and fronting on the Blue Nile.

'Surely,' said Hassan, 'I told you. My great-grandfather was murdered by General Gordon's side, on the steps of the Governor's Palace, not more than one hundred metres from where you are now sitting.'

'No, you didn't, Hassan. Never!' I said.

Why Hassan, who loved a bit of 'theatre' had not made this revelation long before, I couldn't imagine. But now he was launched he went on readily enough.

'One great-great grandfather was a brigadier in the Egyptian army. That was Mohammed el Atabani.'

'Presumably,' I said, 'he was the chap that got killed.'

'He got killed, all right,' replied Hassan, 'but not in Gordon's vicinity. Brigadier Mohammed el Atabani was defending Khartoum Garrison. It was at a battle against Mahdist followers, called the Battle of Messellemiya Gate. You can see the site: a railway passes through it and there are some few graves scattered about it. I will show it to you. The body of the Brigadier was carried by servants and buried in a "gubba". This tomb still stands in the centre of Khartoum.

'You are not absolutely clear,' went on Hassan, 'about our ancestors. It was in fact our great-great grandfather – two greats – who was the Brigadier. It ws his son, Ibrahim Rushdi el Atabani, our great grandfather – one great – who was murdered by Gordon's side. In fact, that was in 1885. The same year when the Brigadier was killed. Father and son. The two in one year. Ibrahim Rushdi el Atabani was First Secretary to General Gordon. According to an eye witness it was he and an Egyptian who were murdered at the same time as Charles Gordon. Of course it is mentioned in the history books. I will draw you a family tree.'

Hassan handed me the 'tree'. Looking at it, I recalled what an illustrious family it was. Hassan's brother, Ahmed, for instance, had been the Sudan's first attorney-general and had written its first Constitution. And one of Hassan's sons, Galal, now represented his country as ambassador in Beirut.

Hassan, it seemed, was enjoying talking, and I certainly wanted him to go on. I asked him about his early days in the Public Works Department, the forerunner of the present Ministry. He told me how, about midway between the two world wars, the building section of the P.W.D. had been started by two British architects, Mr. Bridgeman and Mr. Francis, who recruited two newly qualified engineering graduates from Gordon Memorial College. One of them was Hassan himself; and from Francis he received, as he put it, 'two years' complete instruction'.

'He was a little bit hard,' said Hassan. 'But,' he added quickly (for no Sudanese 'whines' – that I had learned already), 'he had to be hard, one should understand that!'

'I shall never forget one incident,' he continued, warming to his narrative. 'Mr. G.E. Francis had brought me a plan of the Wadi Seidna School, which was then a single storey building. "Now, Hassan" said Mr. G.E. Francis, "I want you to draw a plan for an addditional storey to go above this ground floor plan which I am giving you. The new upper floor plan should be something like the sketch I have made, here."'

Hassan paused to consider how he should explain what happened next. Then he resumed: 'I placed down on my drawing board the plan of the existing ground floor building. Then, when I had drawn the outlines of that building upon tracing paper, I drew within the outlines on the tracing paper an upper storey plan which was made exactly from Mr. Francis's sketch, so that I made a representation of a two-storey building. Then Mr. Francis came and said, "Hassan, you have made a grave mistake."

'I told him: if I knew the mistake, I would have corrected it.

'Then, with a serious look, he replied, "No! You should have to know it." I kept looking at the drawing but never found what mistake I did. Not for the whole day. From eight till two. Mr. Francis told me to go back home and come fresh in the morning and again look at the drawing.'

In Hassan's office, the white wooden shutters excluded much of the glare of the sun. But it was nevertheless very warm. For a time we sat hushed, as though suspended in a quiescent, timeless world. Momentarily I was back in the Derby of my

*17 Sharia el Gamhuria*

childhood. The sun shining. Undisturbed days. A green-painted steamroller moving slowly in an empty street. My perambulator with its four huge, spidery wheels. Memory lurched forward to another scene: Sunday School outings – with stunning girls! And then my mind slowly focussed in imagination on the picture of a sensitive Sudanese and a stern, well-meaning middle-aged Englishman enacting, at some infinitely remote period, a simple, distressing incident. The very one that Hassan was describing. An incident of a kind that arises time and time again, wherever teaching goes on, and which on every occasion is capable of leaving a life-long scar on a youngster's memory. I guessed that Hassan, too, had allowed his mind to turn inward as he re-lived the trauma created by his mistake in planning the Wadi Seidna School.

After a time, he stirred himself.

'I came early the next morning and started gazing at the drawing, and I found the mistake. Wadi Seidna School was built of brick, and in such constructions, as you know, when an upper storey, also of heavy brick, is required the new brick walls should be closely related to the ones that exist. That way they are able adequately to support the upper storey. By sticking too closely to Mr. Francis's sketch I failed to provide for this. So I scrapped my drawing and did another that was correct.

'When Mr. Francis came and looked at it he said, "Now you can rest assured, Hassan, that you will never commit such a mistake again." And suddenly I fainted and fell back from the stool on to the floor, where I knocked my head. I shall never forget how that person, who had been so hard with us, changed to a very sentimental person that particular moment. He took me in his arms and carried me into his office, where he had a thermos flask filled with cold water. He poured the water here' (Hassan pointed to the centre of his pate); 'he stopped more of the blood from coming out and took me to the hospital, where I had two stiches. And after that for four days he kept coming to me and said, "Don't touch anything and rest in your chair."'

With the juices of Hassan's memory now running so freely, I seized the opportunity to ask about the origin of the beautiful University house in which we were then living, 17 Sharia el Gamhuria, a single-storey structure of brick. Its main feature was an open verandah which curved gracefully forward at the centre of one of the longer sides, its lintel supported by six Tuscan columns.

'I,' replied Hassan, using the conjuror's manner to which he so readily resorted, 'I was one of the people who drew it, with Mr. G.E. Francis.'

I told him I was amazed – I had thought it to be much older. But Hassan, who has a precise memory for dates, insisted that this and other houses in the area had been built in 1936. He explained:

'Such Roman columns had been sent from Britain to decorate the streets of Port Sudan when, in 1911, King George and Queen Mary visited the port on their way to India. Later these columns were sent to Khartoum, for re-use in buildings. But Mr. Francis was the first to copy them by reducing their dimensions. We used to draw them full-size,' explained Hassan, 'on rolls of paper spread on the ground. And we used to draw the "entasis" – the outward-swelling part on the middle – with a stick. To make people feel the columns had strength.'

'I know about entases – like we have, Hassan. You and I,' I suggested, pointing below my belt to a handsomely projecting 'tum'.

Then with 'g's hard (as in 'gate'), he used another of those pet phrases that we had already come to relish: 'Just a suggestion'. And we laughed, self-confessed partners in deformity.

'You see,' continued Hassan, 'after the war when Independence was on the scene, they wanted those people who had remained with Mr. G. E. Francis to go abroad and do some courses in architecture. I was already studying here in Khartoum. I had ambitions, so, by correspondence only, I was studying with the Bennett College.'

'Good Heavens!' My astonishment was not exaggerated. 'I remember the old advertisements'. And my mind flew back to those innumerable full pages in the *Strand* or the *Listener*, dominated by the photograph of the benevolent-looking Mr. Bennett himself, with its invariable legend: 'Let Me Be Your Father'.

'But didn't you study in England, eventually?'

'Well, yes,' said Hassan 'I wished very much to have a British qualification, to have the magic initials R.I.B.A. after my name. I heard that the Institute would give a special qualification to those over thirty years of age. So I went to London soon after the war, to study under Mr. Howard Robertson, whose impressive arch-like constructions at the Horticultural Hall, in Westminster, I had seen illustrated. I worked at the Architectural Association School – but for less than a year. For you see, I found out that to be a member of the Royal Institute of British Architects, I must be a British subject. So I quitted my course and came back to the Sudan and joined the Ministry of Works.'

Not long after hearing this tale of Hassan's frustrated hopes, we noticed that Mr. (as he then was) Basil Spence, at that time President of the R.I.B.A., was to visit Central Africa. 'Wouldn't it be splendid,' suggested Margaret, voicing my own unspoken thoughts, 'if we could persuade him to stop off in Khartoum? Wouldn't it be a boost for our students?'

So we wrote, and he came – in March 1959 – accompanied by his wife and the Institute's secretary, Mr. Bill Spragg. He delighted the students by his good-natured criticisms of their drawings and his accounts of the problems he had faced over Coventry Cathedral; and he astonished them by his lightning sketches made with a 6B pencil which he always carried ready for instant use.

A high spot of the visit was a supper party in our garden at 17 Sharia el Gamhuria. Here it was that Basil Spence met Hassan Atabani. They got on famously: a pair of extroverts with an exuberant approach to life's problems, each with a belief in his own ability to solve at least some of its architectural ones! So the next morning, as we tucked into gorgeous Sudanese pink grapefruit, we ventured to raise the question of whether the R.I.B.A. ought not to have an Honorary Corresponding Member in the Sudan. And should the Institute agree to this, whether it would not be more than appropriate to ask Hassan to become the first holder of this office.

Urged by its President, who in turn was supported by the British Embassy and by the testimony of Mr. Roddy Enthoven, an eminent British architect familiar with Hassan's work, the R.I.B.A. reached a favourable conclusion. The news came first to me, and I hastened to tell Hassan. When he realised that neither nationality nor anything else now stood between him and those coveted initials, words almost deserted him. 'Totally O.K.' was all he could answer, but his smile proclaimed his happiness.

'Perhaps – by way of celebration – we might go to see the site of the Battle of Messellemiya. Where Brigadier Mohammed el Atabani was killed defending the Khartoum Garrison. You promised!'

We went! And as Hassan had said there were railway lines, sidings partially sand covered and graves. Stray sheep nibbled at the poor grass between the tracks in this spot where once blood had been spilled.

After that, we were guests in Khartoum North for supper at Hassan's. As ever, the food was delicious. And the 'Ful Sudani' – Sudanese Peanuts – were particularly good. We ate them mightily. And we must have left Hassan in no doubt regarding our appreciation of the fare provided!

I suppose it must have been a week or ten days later we were about to set out for home leave. The early evening we had spent at the University, returning to No. 17 only in time to cook our evening meal. Then, as we approached the verandah we spotted something! A bulging 'guffa' lay on the bamboo table, visible between the

Tuscan columns. Its rounded top was drawn together by stout brown string. Wedged below the 'guffa' where it made contact with the table was a scrap of paper, closer inspection disclosing a written message in a well developed, confident hand:– 'H.M. Atabani'.

The 'guffa' was crammed with 'Ful Sudani'.

'Just another of Hassan's touches!' said Margaret.

## 2 Specialisms of the Sudan

Anyone wandering about in the market areas of Khartoum in the 'fifties could see that the Sudanese were no strangers to the idea of specialisation. With only one or two exceptions shops sold individual products or offered exclusive services.

Nearly every business proclaimed itself by a hand-painted sign projecting at right angles to the facade of the premises. Always individual and sometimes works of art, these signs were quite unlike the plastic glass and neon-lit monstrosities which afflict our own shopping centres. We loved them and made careful copies of the most attractive ones. In keeping with the multi-racial character of Khartoum, the signs mirrored the spelling and pronunciation preferences of a variety of peoples. We soon found the same thing in daily life when, for instance, our Arabic friends would address us as 'Botter', since 'P' is not an Arabic letter nor can it be pronounced by any Arab.

The fact that 'The Modern Factory of El Khazaran' made chairs was not stated in words for English-speaking readers, but the sign made this clear enough in pictures. The 'Bombay Bazaar's Show Pooms' sign was instantly eye-catching for reasons undreamed of by its careful but uncomprehending scribe. And imagination ran riot at the thought of what might accrue from placing a commission with 'Shaaban Abdel Wahab's Painting Workshop for Motor Car.'

Here in Khartoum we were in some ways back in the world of our childhood where 'multiples' were in their infancy and 'supermarkets' unheard of. A chemist's shop was identifiable by its three enormous decanters filled with red, yellow and green liquid. That was where, whatever the illness, you went to purchase THE MIXTURE, prepared, bottled and labelled in the chemist's own back-room dispensary, and deftly wrapped in your presence in fine white paper fastened with a blob of scarlet sealing wax. You didn't go there for typewriters, or books, or gramophones – these were to be found elsewhere, in the stationer's, the bookseller's or the music shop.

In retail trade, then, we found in Khartoum that specialisation was the order of the day. But this was not so when it came to constructing houses and public buildings. As yet, the job of calculating stresses and strains, and that of co-ordinating spaces and providing structures to appeal to the eye and mind, had not been allocated to different professions. Anyone seeking guidance on building matters would turn to a *'muhendis'*. This Arabic word can be roughly translated as 'engineer' – but misleadingly, for it signifies 'a maker of things', like the *'mistri'* in India, rather than any of the multitudinous meanings of our word.

Yet oddly enough, the British architect of Khartoum Palace was an engineer who converted himself into a *'muhendis'* and even, it must be said, into an architect, the creator of this dream of white arcades, massive external flights of steps and pleasantly shaped windows enriched during our time with duck-egg blue paint, which still stands proudly in the heart of the city. It was Kitchener himself, a few weeks before he became the Governor-General of the Sudan in 1898, who appointed the young Lieutenant Gorringe as architect of the Palace. The fact that Gorringe had not passed any architectural examinations was a small problem. Ever resourceful, Kitchener handed him a selection of past papers, suggesting that when he had a look at them he might care to set one for himself. This met with an immediate and discerning response. Not only did he set the examination, he passed with flying colours.

Thereupon he rose to the rank of captain and sent for architectural books from England. As he himself was to put it, with all modesty, 'With the help of these plans, elevations and other architectural details which they contained, I designed ... the new Palace.' And having, so to speak, developed a taste for this particular kind of work he went on to design a variety of large public buildings fronting on to the Blue Nile.

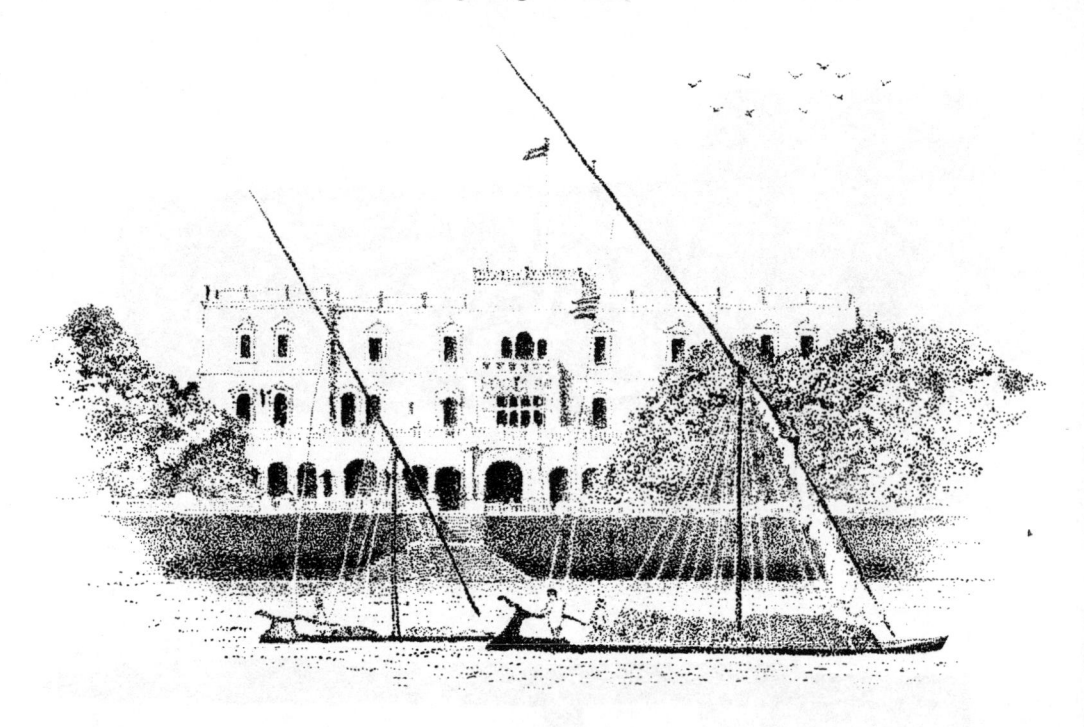

In England, where a degree of job specialisation in the building industry had emerged in the early decades of the nineteenth century, becoming firmly established by the beginning of the twentieth century, it did not escape the notice of at least one of the architectural fraternity that an engineer – a 'stress and strains' man – was doing what could only be called an architectural job in Khartoum: the designing of the Palace.

Calling himself 'Eureka', he wrote a letter to *The Building News* which was published in August 1902 under the heading 'A New Style'. It is a remarkable tribute from a professional to the work of non-professionals – and possibly this accounts for his using a *nom de plume*:

*'Khartoum and its Palace*
The first sight of Khartoum from the river comes as a charming surprise after the long journey through a thousand miles of barrenness, for it is embosomed in trees. The Palace, a massive building, is a finished structure of great durability and elegance, and gives the impression that its builders have come to stay. No professional architect was employed; it is in fact a new style, – an invention of the Royal Engineers. These ingenious officers were quartered here, and got the job to do as part of their duty, and did their best. The result is charming and original. But engineers have to be ubiquitous, like their motto, ('everywhere where right and glory lead'), and those who commenced were not allowed to finish the building. The lower stories are the design

of one engineer, the upper of another, and yet the whole is congruous.

The *Ultima Thule* has been arrived at in an unexpected quarter, and let us hope that the scientific corps will favour the profession with an illustration of what is accomplished in Darkest Africa.'

Gorringe was also employed on the first Gordon Memorial College building, the beautiful structure which today forms the heart of the University of Khartoum. The ground plan was prepared by the architect to the Khedive at Cairo, Fabricius Bey, and on this basis Gorringe built his splendid 'Islamic' arcades and vaulted ceilings. It was in this building soon after our arrival I found myself explaining to a crowded audience of budding *muhendiseen* a new and somewhat revolutionary idea. This was that henceforth those studying building should be divided into two groups, the architects and the civil engineers. The former would be concerned primarily with the social and aesthetic aspects of design, the latter mainly with the ever-increasing problems of strength and stability.

In the early years of the Anglo-Egyptian Condominium an educational system had been set up which concentrated mainly on the elementary levels. But the Sudanese quickly showed an aptitude for higher education; and with the extension of railways, irrigation, telegraphs, and harbours that followed the Great War, there came a clear demand for more highly skilled engineers of the British kind. This led to the establishment of an Engineering High School in Khartoum and the introduction of scholarships to enable Sudanese to qualify abroad for engineering degrees. Those who held such degrees usually specialised in one branch – electrical, mechanical, civil or hydraulic engineering – but they all considered themselves *muhendiseen*.

What I was now proposing to my assembled students, therefore, was that a new profession – that of architect – should now grow up in the Sudan alongside the well-established profession of engineer. This was not simply an idea of my own – it was part and parcel of the many changes on which the country was then embarking. The previous year, 1956, had seen the coming of Independence, with the new blue, yellow and green striped flag and a lively national anthem in march time among its outward symbols. Six months later, Gordon Memorial College became the University of Khartoum; and almost immediately a number of senior Sudanese engineering graduates urged that the time was ripe, if not overdue, for the setting up of a Department of Architecture in the university.

So my first task was to plant the idea of 'architect' in soil where it had scarcely grown before. Many of our potential students, especially in the more remote areas, could have little idea as to the nature and scope of the courses we had in mind. So as a start, we primed them with a little information and invited them to tell us – largely in their application forms – about their home background, interests and aspirations.

Muttalib Balla Ahmed of Ed Dueim district wrote that if he became an architect he would: '. . . receive training in an artistic career which is concerned with making life comfortable and joyful.' A boy from Gereif village had in mind: '. . . to study all the climatic, social and economic factors and to wring from them things of value to the general public.' And still another felt that: '. . . architects are among the poets, artists and the ones who guide and lead the people. They are in contact with the people, serving their needs in all aspects of life.' Inevitably some artless souls described themselves as '. . . fond of beauty' or used equivalent phrases; in others I detected the seeds of business acumen – such as the one who considered it would do his prospects no harm by having a brother already functioning as: '. . . a good local builder.' We had a lad, too, who came from a property owning family. 'They,' he told us, 'spend much of their leisure discussing how to cope with problems of repair.' Just like us! And there was the young gentleman with an address: c/o Barclays Bank, Atbara. 'The architect,' he admonished, '. . . must think in pounds. Lack of money will not allow people to think in terms of sophisticated taste for comfort, good houses or a beautiful environment. Therefore the architect should give easy and economical solutions to the problems of housing.' It might have been our own bank manager addressing us in the Portman Square branch!

Noticeably it was the boys from the most outlandish places who wrote with the most idealism and fervour and possessed the greatest faith in their chosen profession. Bernard Boda Gette, whose house in a village near Wau was: '. . . built using mud made into sun dried bricks with a roof thatched with grass' had a desire '. . . to become an architect to go and help people to construct better buildings which can stand against strong winds and heavy rains.' Adam Ibrahim el Hag of Nyala had a home of stones 'arranged in a cylindrical way with some wood put as a support for the grass which is used as a roof.' And, underlined: 'I want to be some use in my very remote district.'

From such beginnings the idea of the architect's profession as distinct from that of the engineer began to take shape in the Sudan. But *muhendiseen* continued to cover a vast range of activities, and very soon this gave rise to problems. For instance, one of our junior students who travelled to university from his distant home in an open truck, in company with a mass of other folk, indignantly remarked: '*Muhendis* is quite misleading, because it means merely engineering!' It seems that something had gone wrong with the lorry engine, and because someone had rumbled that he was a *muhendis* he was expected to put it right. Senior students saw the problem in a more professional light: 'I disapprove of the word *muhendis* being applied to architects as well as engineers, because *muhendiseen* have been and still are aggressively doing the job of architects. I feel the time has come when each professional has to do his exact job.'

Naturally, civil engineers in our Faculty of the university did not always see eye to eye with this suggestion. Designing buildings paid well! The Dean of the Faculty was an elderly British bull-dog of an engineer who had a lot of army as well as academic experience. To him, architects were a bit of a puzzle. He could not resist the occasional 'dig' – as when, with disarming smile and a wicked twinkle in his eyes, he made his own contribution to a discussion of methods of selecting architects:

'Don't know how you'll sort your chaps out, Potter . . . stick a few bluebells in a pot! Get 'em to draw 'em?'

To a man, the engineers rocked with mirth, those who could visualise 'dark bluebells drench'd with dews of summer eves' and those who hardly knew there was such a flower.

But it was the same Dean who one day breezed into my office.

'Been thinking, Potter. Your chaps aren't engineers. Why, their lectures on first year mechanics – all baby stuff. Ought to change the name of the Faculty. Make it Engineering *and* Architecture. You're not engineers, you know. Bring it up at the next Senate!'

And off he went, this dynamic, kindly, astute septuagenarian. But he was back for a split second, poking his head round the door:

'Go down like a dose of salts – you'll see!'

Up he brought it, and down it went – just as he had predicted. And soon afterwards a change in the terminology took place: architects were now referred to as *mimaryeen* with (but often without) the prefix *muhendiseen*. They were well on the way to becoming even more specialised than the Bombay Bazaar's Show Pooms and no less monopolistic than that ace of practitioners, Sayed Shaaban Abdel Wahab, the proprietor of the Painting Workshop for Motor Car.

It was natural enough to wonder if their newly-created distinction would lead to rivalry and acrimony. But happily things took quite another turn. Even before we left the Sudan on the completion of our work, a graduate architect confided to us: 'I would like to make a team, because a team of specialists can produce nicer and more efficient work'; and another, in a letter we received while on vacation in U.K., wrote of 'the great family of *muhendiseen* and *mimaryeen*'. In our few years in the Sudan we could only lay foundations; but when we heard and read such things we dared to hope for good things in the future.

And what a future, full of unpredictable possibilities, lay before our students, their country, their part of the world! Think for a moment of Bernard Boda Gette, the boy who came to us twenty years ago from his home of mud, poles and thatch in the remote village close to the equally remote town of Wau. The news is: oil discovered in adjoining Province ... so far in small quantities.

# 3 Roots

There was a quietness about Sayed Ibrahim's office which was not merely absence of noise. Indeed, if you listened carefully you might just hear the murmur of air from a concealed cooling system. But Sayed Ibrahim had the ability to create around him an atmosphere of calm and tranquillity. This was his greatest gift, but in addition he was highly educated, as befitted the general manager of a bank.

Sparse in detail, simple in colouring, the scene comes effortlessly before the mind's eye. There he sits, in the less comfortable of two chairs (his visitor has the one with the arms), behind a table which completes the furnishing of his white-walled room; a tall man in his fifties, with a handsome profile and the deep brown colour that is characteristic of the Northern Sudanese.

The business part of our conversation, concerning proposals for a new bank building, had run its course, and now we sat sipping ice-cold *lemoon* from crystal glasses. Our conversation turned to Nubia.

'I come from Nubia – perhaps you know that. I was born in a tiny village close to Wadi Halfa. Like all Nubian villages, it was not much more than a collection of mud houses...'

Sayed Ibrahim paused.

'... with a mosque, mud like the rest.'

He smiled and looked at me shyly.

'Perhaps there would not be much about such places to interest an architect.'

Then he went on, fluently and without hesitation.

'The Nubian villages all lie some way back from the Nile, so they don't occupy the fertile ground close to the river. There is little enough of such ground, in all conscience. It is not a rich country, as you may know.'

He smiled as he painted in the details.

'Of course, we grow palm trees – like most country folk – partly for their fruit and partly for poles. We need poles for roofing our houses. And there are green vegetables, mostly beans; and we have enough to keep a few sheep and goats. Behind the houses the sandy stony ground rises, gradually at first later more steeply, until we get to the *jebels* – the flat-topped hills which are a feature of our landscape.

'One evening my mother was sitting with me up there, on the sand below the *jebels*. The shadows of the houses below were already lengthening in our direction.

'It was a good time for talking. The sun's heat had diminished and the chilling air was yet warmed by that more temperate heat emitted from the earth. And there was much for us to talk about. In particular, mother burned with curiosity concerning my recent travels in Europe. In fact it was the first time I had been to England.

'"Tell me son," she said, "about your travels. Was it far, the place to which you journeyed?"

'"Yes mother, very far," I replied.

'"Then, tell me son, is it as distant as Mecca? – for that too is a far place."

'"Yes mother, further even than Mecca."

'"Son, then you have been to Mecca. How was Mecca?"

'"No mother, I was not in Mecca."

'"Tell me son, how can this thing be? You say the place to which you have been is further than Mecca, yet you were not there! How can this strange thing be?"'

Sayed Ibrahim's voice was soft now with affection.

'You see, mother was very old. When she was a girl there were no schools in Nubia. So it was difficult for her to understand. I tried to explain. I think it eased her mind. And then she put another question:

'"Are they beautiful these far places that you have visited – are they as beautiful as our village, our river and the palm trees?"

'For a time I did not know how I should reply. I thought long. I brought to mind the vine fields of Italy; the rice growing Po valley. These I held in the scales. I added the lush greenery of France and the English pattern of hedgerows. All these I balanced with that which lay before us. Toward the horizon the sky had assumed the colour of ripe *lemoon*, above was like the embers of a huge fire, all around the sands were purpling. Cultivations were at their greenest, pitted with shadows. Below each palm, upon the purple sand, lay an ink black star. Tall women, black robes sweeping behind, carried water in jars upon their heads. Then I knew how I should reply:

'"No mother! To my eyes, this which we see before us is more beautiful than all those places."

'She looked happy – and so, together, we returned to our home.'

# 4 The Finger of Allah

*Act One – Hall of Success*

The Sudan set us one of the greatest challenges of our professional lives – the design and construction of a new examination hall for the University. It had to be capable of seating five hundred students at widely spaced individual tables, overlooked from one vantage point. In addition the hall would be used for large public gatherings, and it had to be capable of being subdivided to enable several lectures to go on simultaneously.

Even by European standards of the day, any building to serve this purpose had to be a big one. By those then existing in Khartoum it was a leviathan, and though – during its gestatory period – heads shook with mistrust, later it became a source of favourable comment continuing long after it was built.

And how *was* it to be built? Thereby hangs a story – indeed a whole string of stories. But as a prelude, here is a description of the building as it was conceived.

'Its construction is both striking and unconventional. Despite the large area it covers, the floor space is uninterrupted by columns – a striking feature in any building but especially so in the Sudan, to which Islamic dome construction never penetrated.

Overhead, too, there is nothing of the routine dome and arch, beam and column; instead there is only an undulating canopy of rich brown mahogany which serves both as roof and ceiling. The second principal component of the design consists of four huge Islamic calligraphic texts, three black and one scarlet, painted directly on the white walls; and – as our story will tell – in a curious way the building of the mahogany roof owed much, and perhaps all, to the introduction of these texts.'

For the Sudan, a hall of such size was a new concept. Air conditioning there was in its infancy, and all large scale gatherings took place out of doors in the cool of the evening. That was the time for cinema shows, degree ceremonies, student musical parties and social functions. Even in our hall the air conditioning was rudimentary; it depended mainly on a scheme of cross ventilation assisted by a few pedestal fans, together with a few other structural devices due to flashes of inspiration that came at vital moments while building was going on!

If the size and function of the new building offered an exciting challenge, so too did the site. Those who go to the examination hall today find it within the nucleus of the original Gordon Memorial College buildings, the foundation stone of which was laid on 5 January 1899 by Lord Cromer, Britain's Consul-General in Cairo. The setting is magnificent. The planners at the turn of the century did not merely build a college, they embowered it in groves of high-domed neem and pointed the way to its main building by a triumphal arch of royal palms. Yet all this care in landscaping had still left room enough for the new hall to sit in neighbourly ease, its curving roof lines and brick walls holding quiet converse from many a viewpoint with the bleached, brown arcades and columns of the College.

Sometimes fate and circumstances conspire, the one presenting a challenge and the other providing the means of responding to it. So it happened to us – not merely once, we felt, but again and again from beginning to end of this extraordinary undertaking.

To begin with, where was the inspiration to be found that would be the germ of the design work? We did not need to seek for an answer – it was already pounding in our heads. Only shortly before the go-ahead for the examination hall was given, we had made a quick visit to Turkey. Working in an Islamic country, we reasoned, it would surely be desirable to know at first hand, and be able to describe with the burning enthusiasm that comes only from personal experience, the fabled treasures of Turkey's Islamic art and architecture. So one fine spring morning we found ourselves cruising over Cyprus, with Nicosia crystal clear fourteen thousand feet below; then a few minutes later the jagged Taurus mountains looming up blue-white with snow. Cloud deprived us of the eagerly anticipated view of Bursa, Istanbul and the Sea of Marmara from the air, but by then we hardly cared. For at that period it was to Lucullus rather than Laker that airlines looked for inspiration. Caviar, eggs (stuffed, like the passengers), smoked salmon, potatoes, peas, chicken, rice, cake – all this, and 'seconds' too, was washed down by white wine, red wine, coffee and whisky.

Yet the real feast, of unexpected richness, came after landing. We were spellbound by the mosques of Istanbul and Bursa in which, beneath vast domes supported

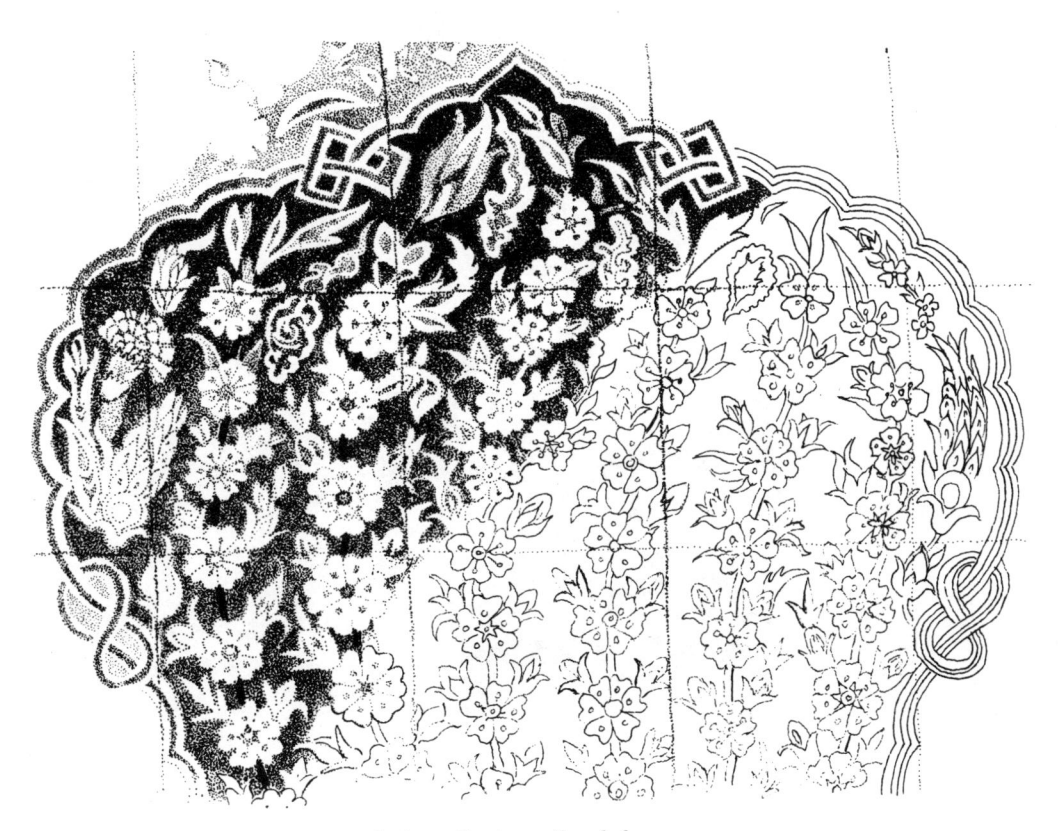

*Antique tiles in an Istanbul mosque*

improbably by thin peripheral structures of arches upon gigantic piers, amazing volumes of space had been imprisoned for centuries. Outdoors, every skyline was pricked by minarets, and wherever we looked the turquoise greens, prussian blues and tomato reds of antique tiles decked tombs and walls, palaces and mosques. But the most exciting discovery of all was Islamic calligraphy, which we were able to study not only in manuscripts but almost everywhere we looked, so commonly was it used as an element in the design of buildings.

The Prophet Mohammed had counselled against representation of men and animals, and in general his followers observed this recommendation. This led to the rejection of the graphic arts for the portrayal of their holy stories. Instead they favoured the dispersion of religious information by means of 'word-painting'. Hence the multitude of Koranic texts which – through the medium of ceramic tile and paint – enrich buildings throughout the Muslim world. Our visit to Turkey brought this home to us. And in Bursa particularly the sheer beauty of the Arabic calligraphy we observed deeply impressed us.

Bursa lies about sixty miles south of Istanbul, a few miles inland from the south shore of the Marmora Sea, which separates Europe from Asia. Since ancient times it has been a meeting point for West and East and famous for its silks and weaving. It was the first capital of the Ottoman Empire, and many religious communities established themselves there, endowing the town with many splendid mosques and shrines, and imparting something of their sanctity to the city itself. To us the finest of all these religious buildings was the 'Great' or Ulu Cami Mosque. Built in the fourteenth century largely to the order of the portentously named 'Thunderbolt' Beyazit, this is essentially simple in form, consisting of twenty large domes (five rows comprising four domes in each row) supported on external stone walls and twelve large square piers. It is these piers which provide the main background, of pure white painted plaster, for the huge jet-black 'word-paintings',* some as much as three metres in height. Some of these calligraphic designs were composed with symmetry as their

* 'Word-paintings' – usually Koranic texts (*sura* or verses). Traditional artistic freedom may make calligraphy difficult to interpret.

*Bursa, inside the Ulu Cami Mosque*

prime objective, for the two halves of the image are mirrored about an imaginary centre line. But even those which are asymmetrical give an impression of perfect equipoise. How these designs, and the aesthetic underlying them, would have gladdened the heart of Leon Battista Alberti, that Florentine architectural pundit of the fifteenth century whose definition of architecture is written on the minds of so many students of our generation: 'A harmony of all the parts ... fitted together with such proportion and connexion that nothing could be added, diminished or altered but for the worse'!

All too soon we were back in Africa, our momentoes of Ulu Cami a couple of browny-yellowy postcards and three or four pages of sketches of the calligraphy. But in addition we had an enthusiasm to share these lovely murals with 'our boys', and a secret ambition to incorporate such pictures as soon as possible in an actual structure. Little did we realize that within three weeks of our return a parcel of requirements would be lying on my desk, to be translated into drawings and specifications for a building.

The day following my appointment as architect of the examination hall a financially hard-pressed government totally prohibited the import of foreign building materials. In theory this was something to be welcomed, since it would place renewed emphasis on the Sudan's immemorial earth-based building techniques. But it was disconcerting to reflect that these amounted to no more than soft Nile brick, palm frond and log, camel dung and hardwood. All save the last had been employed to good effect, but only in small-span construction, and it was extremely difficult to conceive how they could be adapted to the roofing of a large open space.

Faced with such a problem (though never on the scale we were thinking of) British architects in the Sudan had relied on imported cast iron girders as supports for brick vaults. This form of construction, used in Gordon College, dated back to the spinning mills of early nineteenth century Britain. So, of the meagre choices now available to us, hardwood seemed to offer the only solution. But just *how* should we use this material which, in the Sudan, had so far been employed for railway sleepers and little else? This was the question that we carried back with us to London, to discuss with Ezra Levin on our next home leave a few weeks later.

Ezra was Chief Architect of the Timber Research and Development Association, an old friend whom we know as an unfailing source of bright ideas, inventiveness and enthusiasm. He rapidly came up with the answer. This was, he said, a new technique, already tried but still being further developed by the Association, which used laminated boards as roofing members. Like an egg, such a roof was thin but strong owing to the fact that it was curved not merely in one but in two dimensions – hence it had become known as the 'shell' method. But the term was somewhat misleading: the 'shell' obtained optimum strength when the curvature was in opposing planes, one hyperbolic and the other parabolic, so that the resultant form was more like a holly leaf than an egg shell. Thanks to this technique, said Ezra, we would be able to harness the under-utilized timber resources of the Equatorial Sudan to our problem of roofing the great uninterrupted area required for the examination hall.

It did not take me long to realize however, that the shape of this 'shell', based on a geometry which doubtless in many minds – my own not excepted – had become hazy with the years, was not easy to envisage and would be far from easy to describe. My thoughts leapt forward to the explanation I would have to make to the University's Building Committee; and as imagination dwelt even more apprehensively on the task of unfolding the plans to Sudanese building contractors, pessimism deepened to gloom.

Ezra suggested, however, that we should visit a recently constructed 'shell' building in Essex, taking with us the registrar of the university, who happened to be in London on official business – and who, by another happy coincidence, was a member of the Building Committee.

Sayed Ahmed el Mahdi Gobara – for such was the registrar's name, not only rearranged his crowded time-table to suit our suggestion, but also managed to persuade us that nothing would please him more than an excursion to the wilds of Essex. So on a Friday, following the precept 'the better the day, the better the deed' (for Friday is the Islamic eqivalent of our Sunday), we travelled through London's less salubrious eastern quarters in torrents of rain which soon penetrated the car's window frames, formed rivulets down its interior and lay in pools around our feet.

The building we had come to inspect was a school. On entering we gazed up at the 'shell' which formed both ceiling and roof of the assembly hall. Looking at the yellow, shiny surface I felt a sense of anti-climax. Quite unreasonably I had been expecting to see at least a hint of that glowing, matt-surfaced, rich brown immensity of a roof which had begun – no doubt partly under the influence of Ezra's enthusiasm – to take root in my imagination.

Happily my personal feelings of disappointment did not seem to be shared by Mahdi, who surprisingly and to our delight, took chalk and wrote on the blackboard: 'Greetings to the boys and girls of this school from the University of Khartoum' – in Arabic naturally! What fun! Mahdi chuckled, imagining the kids' surprise when they trooped in on Monday morning for assembly.

At the inquest following our return home the omens must have appeared favourable, for we started work immediately on an outline scheme. It proved impossible to finish this before the end of our leave; but thanks to Ezra, who nobly volunteered to complete the drawings himself and put them on a plane, the precious parcel was in our hands within four days of our arrival back in Khartoum.

Which was just as well, for we found that the heat was well and truly on – both literally and figuratively. Temperatures, and expectations, were running high. There was now some urgency about providing evidence that the plans for the Hall were taking shape. It was necessary, too, to try to work out some preliminary estimate of cost. I well remember how, when I approached Sayed Hassan Atabani, the chief architect for the Ministry of Public Buildings, for help with this, he remarked how brave we were – attempting in Khartoum something that nobody in their right minds would think of. This, I decided, was to be taken as a compliment, and I thanked Hassan accordingly.

He went on to remind me that there would have to be a meeting of the Building Committee – of which he was a member – to give final sanction before work started. Of course, of course . . . but under stress of the intense heat and long hours of toil, far removed from Ezra's sustaining and moderating influence, my faith in the hyperbolic-parabolic thesis had begun to show signs of fraying. There had been the unfortunate conversation, for instance, with the Professor of Engineering Mathematics, when I

*White Nile steamer passing through The Sudd swamps carrying cargo of mahogany planks*

explained the principles of our design, only to be told he hadn't the remotest idea of what I was talking about! I began to hope that a vague rumour I had heard, that Arabs tended to be particularly sensitive about losing face by revealing the limits of their knowledge, might lead the Building Committee not to probe *too* deeply into the plans and the ideas underlying them.

But there was now an even more immediate worry.

'Alick,' said Mahdi Gobara, 'I am doubtful if we can count on the timber from the South being here in time.'

By now I realised that all our timber would have to be transported by river steamer from Juba, a thousand miles away up the White Nile. That meant going through the Sudd swamps, where water hyacinth and papyrus plants were multiplying to block the waterways as never before. And Mahdi had another mournful reminder:

'Not a piastre over £S.20,000 for the job.' By this he meant the *whole* job, I should explain. So it was not surprising that soon, in one of my letters to Ezra, I found myself predicting that we might have to settle for sand floors and no electric light.

Obviously, every possible string had to be pulled. As to the timber, for instance, clearly a personal approach had to be made to the Minister of Agriculture who, since the revolution, was also Minister of Transport and therefore responsible for trains, camels, donkeys – and river transport. Then there were dozens of points of detail which had to be settled before that momentous meeting of the Building Committee – temperature control was just one of them. I pondered over our calculations: the body heat of five hundred chaps in the Hall, even without making any allowance for examination fever, might be equivalent to about 125 two-kilowatt fires. As I sat pounding my sweat-sodden typewriter, the thought seemed hardly bearable.

*Papyrus plants*

The Building Committee which was to have put an end to indecision and doubt did no such thing. It was long, and it was inconclusive. It lasted from ten in the morning until two in the afternoon; and a good deal of cold water was thrown on the project.

'It will never last', I was told.

'The waterproofing will tear as the huge area of the roof rises and falls according to temperature changes', said another.

'It will never get built in time'; and then, worst of all:

'They'll never be able to make it here' – a prediction which cut uncomfortably near the knuckle.

By contrast, the Vice-Chancellor, who was in the chair, exuded a quiet optimism and confidence. He talked of the University giving a lead to the country and answered the doubters firmly: 'I understand from Professor Potter that all these questions have been carefully considered and taken into account in the design'. As he delivered his summing up, I gazed fixedly at the olive-wood table top before me.

Arriving home after three o'clock for lunch, feeling pretty cracked up, I was soon embarked on a letter to Ezra in which I threatened to 'pack the whole thing up.' A childish outburst, but the 'London Office' was able to read our minds from the P.S.: 'Message from Margaret – can you buy her a garden sprinkler. It's to fit the end of a plastic hose – inner diameter half inch – and should be of the twizzle type.'

The next day we felt we had to put the record straight. So off to Ezra went a new bulletin:

'Feeling better today. Goodness knows what's happened to the weather. It's the hot season. When we were taking the 'stick-shadow' reading yesterday the sun was slap overhead – a plumb vertical shadow line down our north-south living room wall – at mid-day! And it's not raining, as it should have been weeks ago. This year we only had about ten minutes. My goodness! That storm you had in London made good reading. Everything being wonderfully flooded!'

The thought of the roof now drove us to visit the stockyards of the Forestry Department. Gazing at all that wonderful mahogany and absorbing its perfume, we became intoxicated with the thought: *This is going to be an Important Building*. And we decided that we would order forthwith three thousand pounds' worth of the stuff – just about enough, we calculated, for the entire job. It was our only chance of getting kiln-drying going in Juba soon enough to ensure – we hoped – that the wood arrived in Khartoum when it was needed.

Such a huge bet needed to be hedged, so off went yet another in the stream of letters to Ezra:

'As you'll see from the enclosed, the order has been placed on an entirely unofficial basis – just me buying it. It was the only way to get them going in Juba. So if we don't build the blooming shells, Margaret and I will be setting up in business in Khartoum as timber exporters. And we'll rely on *you* to set up shop in the U.K. to off-load thousands and thousands of threequarter-inch mahogany boards on to the market!'

The order placed, we were not able to get reasonably firm dates for delivery from the Forestry Department. So now we turned to the task of getting necessary authorizations from various agencies and departments of central and local government. It would help our case, we felt, if we were able to demonstrate to the next meeting of the Building Committee that all the hurdles had already been cleared. A scribbled air letter to Ezra put him in the picture:

'. . . they are very hot about all the bits of reinforcement and even ask to see the calculations. I spent a complete day and a half getting rubber stamps on the permits and collecting signatures from government offices all over town. Only the Municipal Engineer is outstanding. But he's very helpful as well as being a good engineer. I think we shall be all right.'

With the timber on order, and a sheaf of permits now nestling in the file, what else could we do to prepare for the day of decision?

'Perhaps', said Margaret, 'if we were to build a really *splendid* model, that – in addition to knowing about the timber and the permissions – would bring us home and dry.'

There was little time before the fateful meeting – too little, it seemed, for the making of a large scale model suitable to place before the Committee. But the effort had to be made. We decided on a scale of one centimetre to one metre (or one inch to eight feet four inches); and for the crucial element of the design, the eight roof shells, we used real mahogany, showing each board of the final structure marked on the inner surfaces.

A rare moment of calm gave us a chance to wing a progress report to London:

'The model's going well. Big pictures we sent show it only half finished, with all the interiors still rough, assembled in an incomplete state for photos. Since then it's been

*The Finger of Allah – Act One* 49

unpicked, worked on and reassembled. Side shells, in particular, with their individual mahogany boards, look super. The four main shells to go into position, temporarily, this afternoon. The Hall platform is in, and – if you please – (what a lark!) a LADY speaker holding forth from the rostrum! Margaret made models too of peanut sellers, students and fat expatriates!'

The model was still incomplete on the eve of the Building Committee meeting, so we worked throughout the night on the remaining details. By now the roof shells were finished, even to the external membrane with which we had covered them to simulate felt cladding. We were happy to think that now the committee members would be able to see at a glance what we were aiming at, with a clarity that drawings and words could never have achieved. Only one small but vital feature was still lacking in this part of the model – a turret which we now cemented to the highest point of the main roof. This we intended as a ventilator and lightning conductor, but on our model it served as an even more important purpose – as the knob, like that of a saucepan lid, by which the roof could be lifted off to display the 'shell' construction and to disclose the interior.

The best of these finishing touches was yet to come; making it consumed the remaining hours of darkness, and at last we climbed the wooden ladder to our open-air sleeping place on the flat roof. The greenish lemon colour of dawn already infused the sky. On the still air came the sing-song chants from within the minarets: 'There is no god but God; Muhammed is the Prophet of God.' We were content, and for a little while we could sleep.

The effect of the model on the Committee went beyond all our hopes. As I walked in with it, a hush fell. I lowered it cautiously on to the table, and then gently lifted the lid off by the turret. All stood revealed: the hyperbolics and parabolics, no longer just mathematical equations and blue-printed lines, had been transformed into shapes as delicate, functional and *real* as the wings of birds. And there was something else, which the hours of darkness had brought to us, and of which we had no inkling the day before: on the white walls at each side of the great open central space were emblazoned gigantic inscriptions in Islamic calligraphy.

Suddenly communication became amazingly easy. I found myself launched effortlessly on an explanation of how this crowning feature in the design had come into being. The decision to decorate the walls in this way had *literally* been made at the eleventh hour – that is, shortly before midnight the previous night. Looking round our bookshelves for inspiration, we had lit on the sketches of word painting we had made in Bursa of the calligraphy in the Ulu Carmi Mosque.

I went on to tell the Committee how Margaret, having perused every one of the sketches – all of them of course, meaningless to us apart from their beauty of form – had worked out a plan of action.

'I'll take a bit from some and bits from others, and weave them all together to make a whole so composed as to look well and fit into the architectural features. There can be a big splotch in the centre and sweeping upward curves at each end to tie it all together.'

Reduced to words, this formula for the inscription seemed hardly a promising one; but when roughed out on tracing paper it looked very good indeed. I was all for painting it directly into position but, cautious and infinitely patient as ever, Margaret had other ideas. She dispatched me into the night with a gentle but firm command.

'Now ... you take the rough, find a student and ask him to turn my meaningless jumble of shapes into something which makes sense but which looks, from a design angle, roughly the same.'

This was a tall order at that hour of the night, but in one of the design studios I was fortunate enough to find Sayed El Amin Muddathir, who was also burning the midnight oil. One of my students, and incidentally a devout Muslim, he quickly grasped what we were after. For a moment he studied Margaret's drawing, and then he beamed at me.

'Why change this? It is perfect Arabic. In fact it is classical Arabic. And I myself would regard it as a most suitable adornment for an examination hall, for its meaning is God is the giver of Success.'

'And so', I concluded to the assembled Committee members, having by now lapsed totally and unashamedly into autobiography, 'I went back home to tell Margaret what El Amin had said. You can imagine how strangely she felt.'

As I talked, I had become aware how intently the Vice Chancellor was listening, and how with every word I uttered he seemed to become more delighted. By now his eyes were shining with merriment, and his good natured face was creased with smiles.

He rose to his feet and spoke.

'Here I detect the Finger of Allah. May I propose emphatically that we build the Examination Hall exactly upon the lines shown here. From now on this Great Hall shall no longer be linked in its title with "examinations". Instead it shall be called THE HALL OF SUCCESS.

*Passengers boarding a White Nile steamer*

# 5 The Finger of Allah

## Act Two – El Hamdulillah

The design of the Examination Hall, its specification, its bill of quantities, were all complete. The necessary permissions to build had been obtained, and the Building Committee had not merely accepted the scheme – it had urged that the model should be put on display as part of the Revolution Day exhibition, and that 'the attention of our honoured guest, President Gamal Abd el Nasser should be drawn to this new and significant building shape.'

The time for argument was over. Now, clearly enough, we were expected to get the job moving as quickly as possible. Our first task was to obtain quotations, or 'bids' as the Sudanese often preferred to call them. And it was no accident that this word, with its overtones of gamesmanship, was used; for the Sudanese, builders and clients alike, regarded building as a kind of game. Play began as soon as the contract was signed. From that moment the contest was one of attack and defence, as the builder tried his hardest to score 'extras' and the client's side fought to contain him.

Our builder, Sayed Gabir Abdul Izz won the contract against competition from five other firms – three Sudanese, one British and one Egyptian – putting in a bid which undercut all others by a wide margin. I felt pretty sure that he relished the idea of mastering a new technique, though I doubted if he fully understood the drawings. What was certain was that his razor-sharp mind and acute business sense would soon be concentrated on the 'extras game', of which he was already known as a star player.

Claims for extra payments could be made on a variety of counts. For instance, it could be argued that the drawings were not being fed through to the builder in time, or that the materials specified and billed were unobtainable – something which could and indeed often did happen in Khartoum at that time. To assess such claims, still more to refute them, might often be no easy task.

That other minds than ours were grappling with the problem soon became apparent to us through the affair of the Great Banian Tree. At one end of the Examination Hall site was the Faculty of Law; at the other was the administration block from which our Registrar, Sayed Mahdi Gobara, controlled the university's finances and performed a host of activities. No one knew better than Mahdi the hazards of building in the Sudan, and above all the penalties that might be incurred by delay.

So, the very day that the contract was signed between the University and Sayed Gabir, the evidence of Mahdi's foresight (as I guessed it to be, and afterwards confirmed) confronted me as I went home for lunch. The great tree lay upturned, its roots silhouetted unnaturally against the sky, a tangled mass of limbs and leaves spreading far beyond the limits of the site. In the adjoining road a line of market drays was being loaded by a multitude of labourers, their orange caps bobbing frantically in the sea of white robes, while between the shafts the draught-mules and donkeys chewed happily away at the unending feast of banian leaves. On every side, people were hacking at branches with any sharp piece of metal they had been able to lay hands on, for in Khartoum wood was a rare and valuable commodity.

For me, the sight of the toppled tree was somehow disturbing. Suppose we hadn't had the benefit of Mahdi's forward thinking ... suppose that in four days' time this giant tree had still been there, with Sayed Gabir's army of building workers taking their expensive ease in its shade! By the foresight of a friendly colleague, this pitfall had been avoided, but how many more lay ahead? Suddenly the life I had forsworn, of operating within the framework of an established architectural practice, stimulated and helped by professional cronies, with expert technical advice almost immediately at hand, seemed to have overwhelming attractions. True, we could always turn to Ezra for reassurance and help when things got tough. But as I trudged homeward, the heat of the sand burning through the soles of my *merkub* slippers, even this thought was depressing rather than heartening; for Ezra in St. John's Wood, London, seemed at the moment to be worlds away.

And then, quite inconsequentially it seemed, an ancient memory flashed into my mind. I saw my old headmaster listening with disapproval and ill-disguised impatience to my attempts at Latin translation.

'Potter,' he was saying, 'what Horace is trying to tell you, but you don't seem to understand, is that *these things in future years it will be a joy to recall.*'

Of course! The heavier the seas today, the more delicious the calm to-morrow. I was grateful to my memory for having made the point in a picture-parable, banal in itself and translated for Margaret's benefit into another banality: 'We must get cracking.'

As usual, she was full of practical suggestions.

'Better get the whole building pegged out on the site – that will give Gabir a good start. To-morrow's Friday; it will be quiet. If we are up by first light, we should finish the job by lunch.'

So it was that, as the sky flushed shell-pink in the direction of Burri Village and donkeys hee-hawed their salute to the dawn, we loaded the university surveying kit into our car: a collection of black, white and red poles, measuring chains, tape, marking arrows, cold chisel and sledge hammer. There is always pleasure in working in the freshness of early morning, but nowhere is it so keenly experienced as in hot, dry lands such as the central areas of Sudan. A mere two minutes' drive brought us to the site. Not a trace of the banian remained; yesterday had indeed been the day of the locust. Now for the first time we were able to see the whole area and take it in at a glance.

A glance was all we gave it, for there was work to do. With sledge hammer and cold chisel I started to make the first hole in the sun-baked earth, in which to fix a surveying pole. Hard work even in the cool of the morning ... and a vision of the labourer's reward floated before me – of sitting semi-recumbent, ice-cold glass of that delicious Camel beer in hand and the crisp bible-paper pages of the overseas edition of *The Times* spread before me....

'Funny', said Margaret half an hour later, as she moved a pole into line, 'funny really, without the banian tree the site looks sort of small. I thought this was to be a big building. Don't you think it's small?'

I felt annoyed, and very hot – far hotter than exertion and the quickly rising sun alone could account for. The plan of the site had been given to us with dimensions marked. We checked and re-checked the measurements on the ground. They didn't agree with the plan. We tried moving the perimeter of the new building. It wouldn't fit. At one point it would collide with the Law Building and at the other extremity with Administration.

'Pity,' said Margaret wistfully, '... about the banian tree, I mean.'

'Oh, damn the tree!... Now the whole University will know. Trees like that aren't cut down without a reason.'

Margaret correctly interpreted my jumbled sentiments.

'People don't notice all that much.' Then roguishly she added, 'Couldn't you just slice off five metres all round? Everybody would just have to sit a tiny bit closer.'

It was a shameful suggestion, but not without its attractions. It deserved to be thought over in calm and solitude. And anyway, it was nearly lunch time.

'I think', I said, 'the quicker we open that Camel beer the better.'

In the blaze of noon we sat at ease in our two nineteenth-century armchairs, the footrests extended. Our two Sudanese cats sprawled in the shade, their brown-black-white flanks undulating rapidly, their paws lifted to catch every vestige of a breeze and their little pink tongues fully extended from open mouths. The air was so dry that despite the coldness of the beer and the heat of the day not a spot of condensation formed on the bottle or glasses.

'No question', said Margaret, 'of bothering Mahdi on a Friday, You'll just have to wait and see.' With that, she got out her patchwork quilt, which had already been under construction for three years.

As Margaret stitched busily away, I mused. The measuring of the site had been done by a Sudan Government agency. We had simply worked from a drawing which it made and supplied to us. But shouldn't we have checked the information earlier? I reflected that there wasn't much point in asking such questions. The fact was that there had been no clearly defined allocation of specific duties and responsibilities, for this would be alien to Sudanese ways of thinking. Making cut-and-dried contracts was a procedure that had been imported for use in exceptional cases. But in general the Sudanese tended to rely on a tradition which was not to be found written in codes and rules but was handed down from generation to generation. The central feature of that tradition, I knew, was that you were expected – indeed, relied on – to do your best. No unions existed to tell employers what they might or might not do with their work force; and likewise there was here no Royal Institute to haul me over the coals if I transgressed or back me up in time of difficulty. All this I accepted: in coming to the Sudan I had chosen freedom. And now I was experiencing the rough edge of that choice.

Rested, calm and cooled, I lay back. Overhead was a profusion of green oranges; tomorrow we would pick them so that Margaret could make marmalade. That would be after I had seen the Registrar. And despite the renewed sense of well-being that I now felt, forebodings persisted that there would be red faces when news broke that a contract had been let to a builder to construct a huge building on a site that would not accommodate it.

At eight the following morning I was waiting in the Registrar's office when Mahdi arrived to begin his week's work. Obviously it wouldn't be right even to mention the infamous site plan. Equally, it would be absurd to disclaim responsibility. So avoiding any kind of comment, I stuck to the facts which I presented with brutal objectivity.

At the beginning of my brief recital Mahdi was smiling. By the time I finished he was laughing.

'Is that all?' he asked.

'El Hamdulillah! Thanks be to God. Now everthing is clear. Since it has been established that the Hall will not suit the original position a new site must be found. Sites there are in plenty. The Sudan is large. There is no problem.'

It was like some master craftsman explaining one of the mysteries of his trade, by easy stages, to an astonished apprentice.

'Together we will go to the Vice Chancellor.'

Side by side we set out, a huge black man with a smaller white man. Both of us wore white open-necked shirts, white shorts and long white socks. But Mahdi was shod in gleaming brown shoes of British leather, while my feet were snug inside my beloved merkub of orange leather from Khartoum's market. Along the central avenue we strode, first beneath the avenue of neem trees and then between silver stemmed palms. Then breathing the perfume from beds of petunias whose blooms reach a prodigious size in that sunny land, we mounted the broad, winding flight of steps which led to the Vice Chancellor's office on the first floor of the old Gordon College building.

It was a wonderful room. In its airy space I always felt the cobwebs of the mind lifting. My affection for it increased as the months became years. The dead white walls; the similarly painted brick vaulted ceiling overhead; the white net curtains ever floating inward on the whispering Blue Nile breeze which entered through the pointed windows; simple wooden furniture – light yellow, the colour of 'fino' sherry. That morning its magic was as good as ever!

As the Vice Chancellor listened, his eyes twinkled. There had been no communication between Mahdi and him before our meeting, but his reaction was just the same as the Registrar's: the smile turned to laughter – even louder than at my first recital.

*Steps leading to the Vice Chancellor's office*

We would have to get a new site. There would have to be a meeting of the Building Committee, of course. Would two days be sufficient for me to prepare new suggestions for the site, with comments on each one?

'Bismillahi – in the name of God – that old building site', said the Vice Chancellor, 'was not the best one.'

His face creased with its customary smile-furrows as we walked out of the room toward the winding steps. Soon I was back home, with Margaret asking eagerly how things had gone. Quickly I told her, and a curious thing happened. She breathed the same response that Mahdi had made when the news was broken to him early that morning:

'El Hamdulillah'.

*A version of 'pit-sawing'*

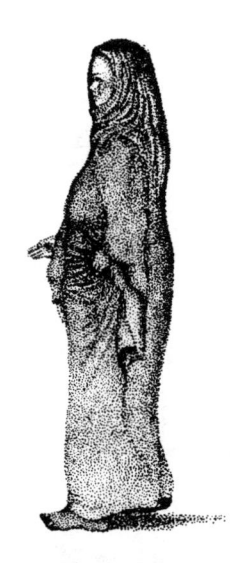

# 6 The Finger of Allah

*Act Three – An Old Woman dressed in Black Rags*

Whatever delays might occur in the building of the Examination Hall, no one should be able to point the finger of blame at the builder, Sayed Gabir. From first to last, he made it clear that this was his ambition, indeed his intention. So, punctual to the minute, he made his entry to the site – and it was a dramatic one. True, there was no ceremony, no band: this was the level-headed Sudan, a country far from the fanatic fringes of religion or politics and dedicated to moderation in all things. Nevertheless it was an impressive occasion. First came Gabir himself, gliding in state in his huge, nearly-new American car. He was followed on foot by a multitude of labourers, mostly from the Southern Sudan judging by their height and the dark colour of their skins, each carrying some kind of primitive tool. An ancient cement mixer was manhandled on to the site. At the tail end of the procession chugged a ramshackle lorry which might have been a relic of the Great War of 1914–18.

Since most of the labourers came from areas very remote from Khartoum, one of the first jobs was to get them housed in temporary lodgings. Within the hour, simple structures were being erected at the edge of the site. They were miracles of improvisation consisting of old packing cases, tree branches, straw and waste building materials. And from the onset a withered old woman dressed in black rags had materialised, as if from nowhere.

It soon became plain that her job was to preside over the makeshift dwellings and attend to the needs of the inhabitants. Every day she could be seen threading her way between piles of bricks and scaffold poles, a stick across her shoulders in the manner of the European yoke, with a five-gallon drum full – now – of water dangling at either side. From time to time a column of smoke announced that cooking operations were about to begin, just as the spreading of clothes on the grass was public evidence of the old lady's labours as laundress.

So long as Sayed Gabir's men were working on the brick walls which made up most of the lower part of the construction, we had no immediate reason to fear there would be any delays for which we could be held responsible. But what was going to happen when the time arrived to start on the roof? No longer would he be using locally produced brick of Nile mud, but those precious mahogany planks I had ordered – a linear mile of planking, if laid end to end, all to be transported a thousand miles down the White Nile. Imagination dwelt anxiously on the paddle wheels thrashing through the two hundred miles of the Sudd's oozing mud and congested masses of water hyacinth. Was there anything we could do to speed the stuff on its way?

Well, we could send telegrams. The forestry people in Khartoum were always ready to send telegrams. When fifty years earlier, the telegraph lines had been installed, no sooner were they up than the elephants knocked them down, while crocodiles habitually devoured the linesmen, and even the operators in their offices were plagued by bats living and dead. Our own wanderings in the south suggested that perhaps conditions had not changed radically: how the service worked was secondary to the fact that it existed.

And how *did* it work? We fell to wondering as we gazed at copies such as this one:

'*TILIGRAM* HARAKA ATBARA 66 UNIVERSITY TIMBER DESPATCHED FROM JUBA VIDE POLICIES 4329 OF 26.12.60, 4233927 OF 27.12.60, 424062 OF 8.01.61 AND 424064 OF 8.01.61 AAA ALL NOT ARRIVED KOSTI AAA PLEASE INSTRUCT YOUR STAFF AT RIVER STATION TO URGE DESPATCH. GHABAT (ON FORESTS DEPT. SERVICES) FOR/ DIRECTOR FORESTS DEPARTMENT. FORESTS/UO/30-G-3/8(a)XR/UO/30G3/5XR/ 1-60/61.

We could make sense of it, of course, but would the recipients in the south be able to decode all those file numbers and understand the message sufficiently well to take rapid and effective action?

These worries grew as the walls rose. Sayed Gabir excelled all our expectations. The fact that his men knew nothing of the wheelbarrow was no impediment. Materials such as bricks, cement, sand and mortar were carried by two labourers, as our ambulance men carry a patient on a stretcher: one man in front, one behind, holding in each hand one end of a horizontal pole, with a pan containing their burden supported between the poles.

Once the walls had risen to full height, timber scaffolding was set up in the interior to form a temporary platform on which the makers of the mahogany roof would work. Poles, planks and logs were bashed and nailed together until the space within the walls was completely filled with a skeleton forest. Vividly it illustrated how ancient Rome tackled the making of the Pantheon dome, or how in Constantinople those

*Calligraphic design for 'Allah'*\*

doughty architects Arthemius and Isodorus carried out the roofing of the Hagia Sophia.

There was still no news of the mahogany, but already plans were being made to celebrate the opening of the Hall. We learned, not without dismay, that thanks to the Goethe Institut, a chamber concert was to be provided by members of the Radio Symphony Orchestra of Cologne.

At this point Nature intervened. Much to my resentment I began to feel unwell and uncommonly sweaty even for that climate. When a red rash appeared and spread over my neck and chest, accompanied by a sore throat, Margaret consulted the 'ailments' section of Mrs. Beeton's *Household Management*. As a result of what she read, a doctor was called in and scarlet fever was diagnosed. This childish ailment proved to be no joke for an adult sufferer. For nearly three weeks I was almost too ill to worry. Then one day, weak and somewhat less strawberry in appearance, I woke to see our site representative standing before me in the middle distance, smiling and holding forth a piece of wood. I took it gratefully, stroked its satin finish and admired the rich plum colour and the gorgeous grain, as the news was given to me that loads of planks were being delivered to the building site. The only problem now, I was told, was where and how to stack it!

At this point the doctor arrived, to prescribe a bottle of ice-cold Camel beer with which to drink the health of the Forestry Department and the telegraph system, who had triumphed over all their difficulties.

Sudan summers are always hot, but that one, with temperatures of 120° F in the shade, was exceptional. Canvas shelters had to be put up to shield the men who were stitching together with nails the three layers of planks which formed the shell roof. But there was still a problem: on exposure to air, the nails soon became too hot to handle. So they had to be poured direct from the packets into bowls of cold water, continually renewed, placed within arm's reach of every workman.

---

\* Some Muslims believe that the name Allah should not be mirror-imaged – as here.

وما توفيقي إلا بالله عليه توكلت وإليه

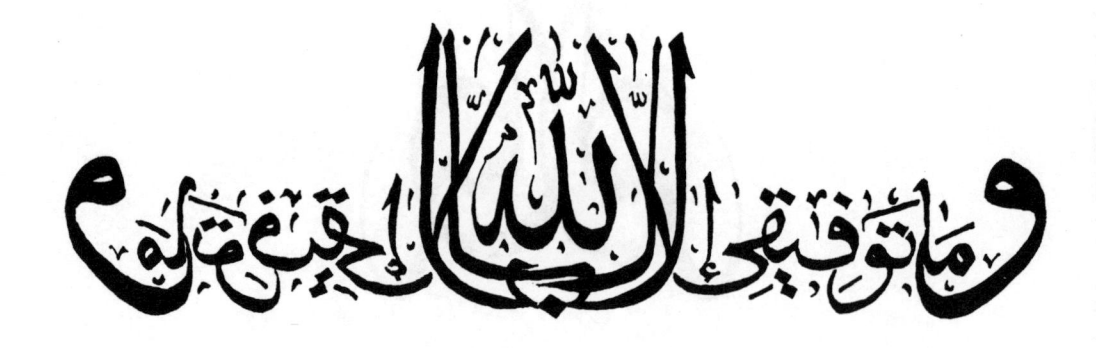

وهو الله ولي التوفيق والحمد لله رب

*Two designs for 'God is the Giver of Success'*

The four great calligraphic designs, which had already played so decisive a part in the Examination Hall's pre-natal history, now seemed to grow in importance, day by day, as critical elements in the design. How were the two matching pairs of inscriptions (one on each of the flanking walls of the central area) proclaiming *God is the Giver of Success* and the other simply the name of God, *Allah* (for use in the smaller spaces) to be transferred from our model to the enormous area of the newly built walls?

After some persuasion, Margaret agreed to execute the full-size versions herself. First, however the calligraphy had to be edited. In Khartoum itself we were fortunate to find a master calligrapher, Sayed Osman Waqialla. It was fascinating to see how, with various sizes of cut bamboos which he dipped in Indian ink, he produced a design for *'Allah'* which instantly pleased all three of us. As for *'God is the Giver of Success'*, he made two attempts. Only with difficulty were we able to make a choice, both were lovely. The selection, finally, rested on the claim that one of them rather better suited the architectural features of the design.

Margaret's task was to enlarge Waqialla's calligraphy from paper-size to wall-size, then line in with paint and finally infill in true signwriter fashion. Against the dead white of the walls, all the inscriptions were to be black – save one of the 'Success' legends which was to be in scarlet, a colour which Mahdi thought would introduce an appropriate touch of cheerfulness!

Every afternoon for over two months Margaret worked on the murals for two or three hours at a stretch, while the rest of Khartoum dozed away its siestas. But there was one exception. There was no sleep for the old lady, tired though she must have been after her morning's toil. Each afternoon, without fail, she stood close to the huge ladder from which Margaret worked, observing every brush stroke. And when the last of the four great murals was completed, she asked for the jars which Margaret had been using to mix her paints and clean her brushes.

With the calligraphy in position and the roof sealed we were at last ready for the fixtures and fittings. We had designed armchairs of yellow *darout* wood, with slatted back panels and smooth hand rests of deep red mahogany. Sayed Gabir manufactured these for us, and a remarkably good job he did, especially in view of the fact that he had never before tackled anything so ambitious in the way of furniture. The caned seats were to be filled with leather cushions, the making of which he entrusted to a group of elderly ladies living in Omdurman. One day he took us in his big, blue, bouncing car to see how work was progressing. The cushions looked splendid, even though none had yet had its stuffing of camel hair. Our ten different arabesque patterns, mostly in green and black, had already been stitched with leather thongs to the cases, which were of that bright orange leather so beloved by the Sudanese for slippers and many other uses. While we were there, the ladies were giving some of the cushions their final polish, rubbing them to a perfect finish with smooth pebbles fished from the Nile close by.

By now it had become clear that the chamber concert would mark the inauguration of the Hall. The date was uncomfortably close; and there was a disturbingly sizeable number of jobs which called for Sayed Gabir's attention – which, we understood, was now being diverted in other directions. There was no electric light, for instance – a serious matter since the concert was to be in the evening. Arabic clock face numerals, which we had drawn full size to be cut from brass in London, were now on the quay at Port Sudan, but transport to Khartoum was impeded by the fact that engine drivers had been sent to Crewe to learn to drive new locomotives. The doors were all secured by string, awaiting locks and handles of the kinds necessitated by their design which were not available locally.

Only with great difficulty were we able to locate Gabir at an address in Old Cairo. Immediately we wrote to him calling for 'a display of industry such as observers of the building scene never previously witnessed in the Sudan!' Then, full of smiles and co-operativeness, he reappeared with magical suddenness. A mighty framework of angle steel grew with tropical speed to form the electrolier equipped with eighty-four fluorescent tubes, which we had designed to hang like an inverted wedding cake from the centre of the roof of the Hall. Sayed Gabir clapped his hands, and lo! – our three great clock faces were cut from aluminium sheets, while a lorry sped to Port Sudan to collect our brass numerals. BOAC and Misrair combined to fly in the door furniture for which we had scoured Sheffield and Birmingham. Finally an army of labourers delved and swept, while others carried away rubbish from inside and around the Hall, every scrap being packed into their *guffa* baskets of palm leaves which they emptied into the bowels of the ancient lorry.

As though to signify the termination of our labours, the weather broke. On the day when, in the morning, the last load of refuse had rumbled out of sight, we stood just after nightfall on the verandah of our house. A hot, damp, dusty smell blew with increasing ferocity from the sandy Batahin wastes and rocky ridges north of the isolated city. A full moon, occasionally visible through billowing clouds showed our paw-paw trees bent almost double by the wind, their finger-like leaves dancing madly. Then the rain came. Dressed still in our flimsy tropical clothes we leapt into our car and dashed to the Hall, eager to see how our monster water spouts were working at

*The night of the great storm*

full stretch. Their function was to throw rain water from the great area of the shell roof clear of the roof sunshades, so that the discharge fell – or so we planned – into water catchers built on the ground below. When we arrived the main catcher, fifteen feet long and shaped something like a great bisected eggshell, was already filled with frothing water into the midst of which a foaming waterfall crashed from the roof above. Mighty noise, motion, clouds of spray – it was fantastic.

By now a thunderstorm was splitting the night sky apart. Gordon College looked like an unearthly and beautiful stage set, before which a double chorus line of royal palm trees lurched and rolled as in a drunken ballet. Already wet to the skin, we plunged in childish glee again and again beneath the delicious, refreshing cataract of tepid water. Only when we were back at home did it strike me that I had forgotten to get Sayed Gabir to make another effort to obtain the copper tape to connect up and earth the lightning conductor on the top of our turret, the crowning feature of our design.

The evening of the inaugural concert saw the Hall filled to capacity. Large sleek black cars nosed beneath the spreading neem trees to deposit 'costly people' of every hue, some in uniform, others in a rich variety of national dress, at the main doors – now happily equipped with handles. One after another they sank on to the old ladies' cushions, to the accompaniment of a soft hissing as air escaped from the camel hair stuffings. Overhead the huge electrolier blazed, while judiciously sited spot lights were beamed on parts of the roof to bring out its curves, shadows and colour. At the back of the stage hung black curtains with Nubian patterns of coloured cloth appliquéd to them by Margaret's hand-cranked Jones sewing machine – whatever would Ma Potter, or Grandma Booth before her, have thought of the idea that their precious machine would ever whirr away at such a task, in such a place, at such a remote period in the future?

But, I mused, the unpredictable is always happening. Indeed, as the Wind Quintet of Radio Cologne emerged in immaculate evening dress from behind the curtain, soon filling the Hall with clearly defined musical sound, I recalled that it had happened that very morning. The leader of the group, Herr Wilhelm Reicha, had remarked on the perfect acoustics of the 'concert hall'. I pointed out to him that it was no such thing in reality, but an Examination Hall.

Smiling yet firm, he insisted: 'My compliments. But, how shall I say, you pull my leg. It is – Concert Hall.'

I was in that state of euphoria in which thoughts fly easily across continents; and by the end of the quartet by Carl Stamitz which concluded the first part of the concert, I was so far away that when the lights went up it was a shock to be back in Africa.

A buzz of conversation commenced but died away almost immediately as the audience became aware of a withered old lady dressed in black rags making her way from the far side of the Hall to where we were seated in the second row.

Erect and proud she shuffled in front of the stage and the very important people. As she approached us we rose from our seats. Silently she took Margaret's right hand in hers, and having raised it pressed it to her lips. Then she turned away, shuffling back the way she'd come. Back across the open area between the platform and the front row of the audience. Back without a glance to right or left. Out through the door and out into the night.

*Flags for a birthday* – the Moolid *(the prophet's). A tent erected as part of preparations for the celebration of the occasion in Omdurman*

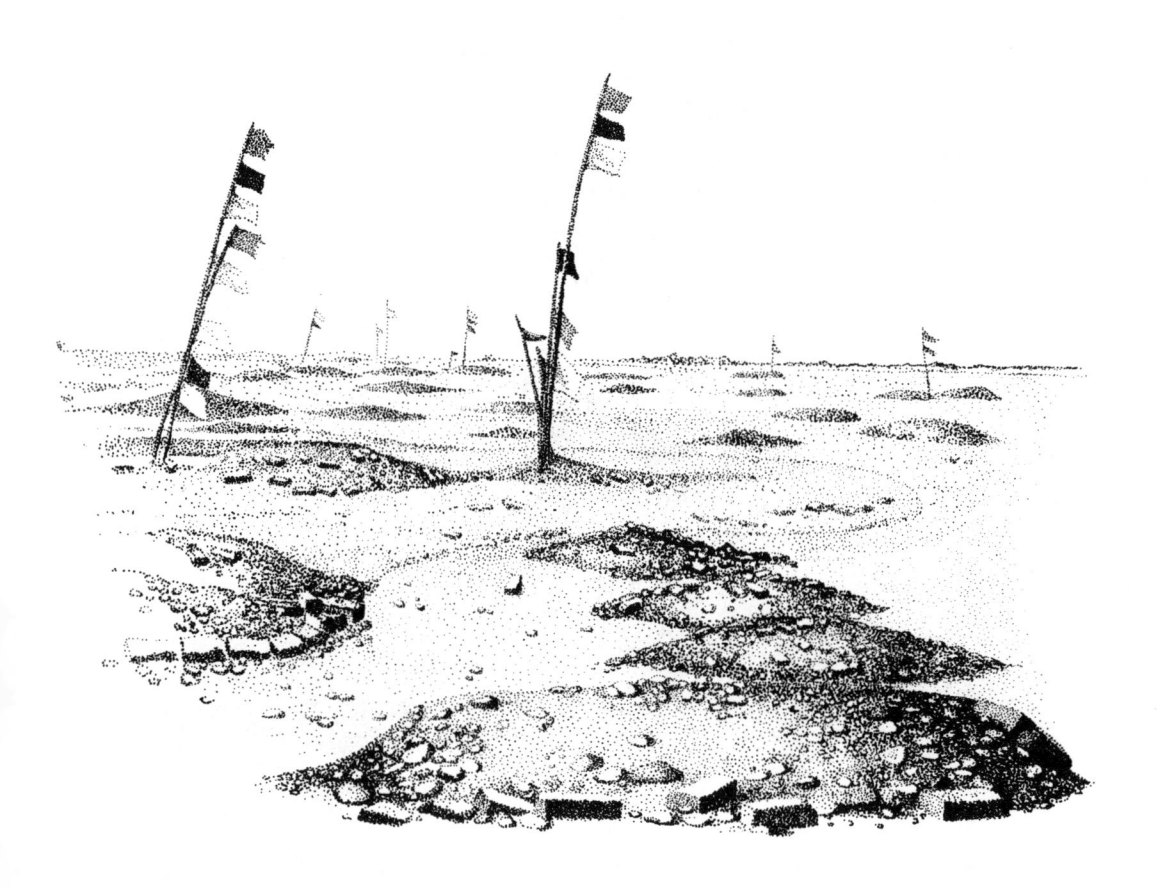

# 7 Travellers in an Antique Land

On the first leg of the journey from Khartoum to Wadi Halfa all went according to plan. We steamed out of Khartoum Station, trundled across Blue Nile Bridge, and headed north along the line skirting Shambat and Salamat el Basha. We noticed from time to time that a little way off from the railway line there were long sticks or poles, bearing flags, pushed into the earth. These marked burial places; they gave a scanty, wraith-like population to the vast empty spaces of the desert. Signs of the living were few and far between: on the furthest fringes of the city a solitary figure astride a donkey rode toward an isolated structure – a mosque from the appearance of its brick walls and decorative pilasters. Later, as the train approached the river, came glimpses of the inhabitants of the villages strung at intervals along its banks.

From the Edwardian comfort of a Sudan Railways dining car, we absorbed the beauty of the Nubian desert, an endless ocean of sand studded with rock islands rising sheer from its surface, their massive heights reflected in the strange blue loveliness of mirages which played continuously amidst them. At last, when our great blue engine had puffed and panted for some six hundred miles, mud dwellings in increasing numbers signified our approach to the frontier town, Wadi Halfa. Funereal symbols were once again to be seen; but there they were not flags flying on sticks but cemeteries of grave mounds, each one covered with pebbles and marked by sticks at head and foot, and each provided with a simple though beautiful earthenware dish for offertory water.

Our objective was Semna East, forty miles south of Halfa. The district commissioner, Sayed Hassan Daffala, kindly lent us a Land-rover to take us along the track which nowadays runs close to the line of the discarded railway built by Kitchener in 1896 to link Wadi Halfa with Akasha. Twisted rails sticking up from the sand and straight ones used as lintels of houses were the sole memorials of the swarming activity that had marked the building of the line and the passage of the troops. Now the land lay stark and silent.

For the most part our track clung to the river's eastern bank, but at times it swung towards the desert. One of these diversions gave us our first sight of Semna East, or Kumma as it used to be called. Half a mile off, at the end of a sandy depression, loomed a high crag crowned by a fort of brick and a temple of stone. Over firm sand we drove to the foot of the crag, and then scrambled to the top.

Before us was an impressive sight – a jagged profile of exceedingly ancient construction silhouetted in black against the silvery surface of the Nile far below. This was the fort, erected some four thousand years ago to guard the frontier of the Egyptian Middle Kingdom, and only a little distance away was the temple. Getting a closer view of the river, we could see how it foamed and tumbled over clean, brown rocks. It is at this point that the Nile cuts through a great rock barrier; here at Semna East, and likewise on the far bank, methodical Nilotic peoples erected military and religious buildings; here, too, their hydrographers measured and plotted the level of the Nile floods, leaving records cut in the living rock, still readable when we came there, but since 1964–65 underwater, flooded by the High Dam.

The temple proved to be a most appropriate place to eat our rucksack lunch. Its interior walls seemed to be covered with carvings, many depicting food and drink – and of somewhat more inviting kinds than the Bovril sandwiches and Lucozade that we were consuming. The likenesses of plump fowls, trussed and obviously oven ready, could be seen cut into the cream-coloured stone. Rows of amphorae, suggestive of delicious and potent beverages, formed the dado decoration. Bewigged humans, frozen for ever in those uncompleted sideways motions so beloved by the sculptors of ancient Egypt, stretched out their hands to pick up drinking vessels and a variety of goodies.

Margaret had been digging into her card index file and now for my benefit she read her notes out loud, enlarging on them as she went. 'The brick fortress is much older than this temple, by many hundreds of years, and people think it was built mostly to the orders of a Senusret king, the Third. His grandfather the First probably had a hand in it. There's a lovely story in Leslie Greener's book, about how Lepsius in the 40s of the last century found two stelae here. One of them was cracked in two and he put each part in a separate crate. But one got left behind here – where we are sitting – and it was another 40 years before another archaeologist, Jan Insinger, arrived on the scene and found the second part all crated up ready for 'off'. That Senusret chap seems to have been a rather nasty piece of work. He seized women, took slaves, wrecked wells, killed bulls and burnt crops. Its all on the stela, which was cracked into two and which was acquired by Berlin Museum in 1899. This Temple is all right though. It was built for Queen Hatshepsut – you like her – but I couldn't find the architect's name! Amelia Edwards came exploring south of Halfa in 1874.'

'So did Albert Tomkins, much more recently, according to the graffito on the rock outside', I replied, as I allowed myself the pleasure of letting my forefinger slide round the profile of one of the amphorae.

When we left the temple we found the wind had got up. The bottom rims of the Land Rover wheels were already covered with dry sand, but underneath the surface was hard, and momentary thoughts of being marooned in the desert quickly vanished. Misfortune was on its way, but not in that form.

It arrived in the dimly lit streets of Wadi Halfa, where we were strolling after a heavy supper of Nile perch. Spells of dizziness hit me; the streets expanded to immense widths, and walls from which I craved support shrank into the distance. Within the outlandish spaces of this Chirico-like townscape, Margaret's voice reverberated strangely, speculating anxiously . . .

'I wonder . . . if you've been eating something that has upset you?'

*Temple wall carvings at Semna East*

Whatever its cause, one thing about this 'illness' soon became clear – its attacks were intermittent. Giddiness was followed by recovery, or at least relief, sometimes for a day or two, sometimes only for a few hours. The sizzling hot trip by steamer down the Nile from Halfa to Shellal was trying; the train journey to Luxor much better. Rashly perhaps we entered the seemingly endless subterranean corridors of the Theban kings' necropolis. They seemed almost as long and confusing as the passages in London's Underground, but not nearly so well lit. There was a sprinkling of 40-watt bulbs dangling by their flex from holes bashed in the vaults of burial chambers, supplemented by other low-powered lights on dusty metal brackets. This dim illumination revealed curious wall paintings, including headless bodies, groping hands and beetles; and its unflattering glow fell on me, too, causing Margaret to say how unwell I looked, and didn't I want to surface?

Arrival in Cairo coincided with further attacks. I lay in bed in a huge, old-fashioned hotel, whose tall French-style shutters closed against the sun's glare and pale walls of French grey wrapped me in calm and seclusion, restoring my spirit and convincing me that I was getting better. Nonetheless we decided to fly straight to Athens, bypassing the Islamic architectural treasures of Isfahan which had been the chief objective of our journey.

Athens brought sustained improvement, and it was even possible to climb up the Acropolis. Possible, but not wise: the old giddiness returned in an acute form. Sprawled on the Acropolis steps, with the Propylea behind us, I became aware of a horrifyingly stormy sky menacing us from across the River Kephissos.

'The end of the world!' I announced to Margaret, inebriated by my giddiness. It seemed as good a place as any, and better than most, for an architect to observe the final cataclysm. But, as usual, she ignored my fantasies.

'We'd better get you to London as quickly as possible.'

We were the only passengers on the plane, so I was allowed to stretch out on the floor on a bed of cushions, with pillows provided and blissfully soft blankets. In London it was the season of pale sunshine and singing birds. Trees in parks and squares were in green leaf – just – each in the hue distinctive of its own species. All this I dimly registered; but I am sure I failed to make the comparison that every other spring brought, between these lime-scented, delicately tinted scenes and the strong brown, plum and yellow of the tropics.

All attention, in fact, was concentrated on tracking down and vanquishing my mysterious illness. So my most clear-cut memories of this time are of what it was to be a 'case'. I see, for instance, a brisk nurse pointing to a cubicle.

'Get stripped! Your kit's inside.'

The 'kit' proved to be a kind of mini-apron reminiscent of the garb worn by the figures I had seen carved on Semna East Temple. As I struggled to tie the tapes round my waist I concluded that this garment was really intended for a much smaller figure than mine.

'Ready, please?' came the nurse's voice.

The Specialist was waiting. He indicated a couch – rather lofty, it was, and not particularly easy to get on to.

'Just stretch out full length!' All very matter-of-fact.

Once attained, my new position gave me no little anxiety. Not only had a bright light been swung into position overhead so that the peering medical students and their mentors could better observe the spectacle, but in addition I felt a chilliness which made me suspect that the tapes had ridden up my waistline – doubtless as a result of my exhibitionist leap up to the couch.

'Now,' said the Specialist '... What's been happening to you? And where did it begin?'

The circumstances of the moment did not favour clear thinking. In a somewhat hazy fashion I recalled Semna East, bas reliefs of banquets, and real Bovril sandwiches and Lucozade. Prompted by such memories, the story of my illness unfolded from Wadi Halfa to West Kenginston; and I noticed with gratification that as I told it, attention seemed to increase.

'Now,' said the Specialist '... I want you to relax. Just lie back and close your eyes.'

I did.

There was a twang. Something cold, metallic and apparently vibrating with great rapidity was being applied to a tender inner part of my nostril. The looked-for reflex action followed. My body sprang into the air.

'Sorry about that,' the Specialist said '... there has to be an element of surprise, you know. Nothing amiss in that department, anyway.'

It was also noticeable that the medical students and the probationer nurses, too, were delighted by the manifestly successful outcome of the experiment.

'It's a most unusual case. If you are no better in a month's time you must come back here. We'd have to try again.'

The days passed. The trees in Regent's Park took on the rich green mantle of midsummer. When it was sunny I managed, with a little help, to ascend the gentle grass and clover slope of Primrose Hill. From its summit I could see, in the blue distance beyond the foreground foliage, the dome of St. Paul's, still undiminished then by the chunky skyscrapers that have since surrounded it, still reigning over the spires of city churches which lie now immured within the glass and concrete.

When the Specialist's month had but a few days to run, suddenly I knew that the aggressor who had fought so hard for the possession of my being was on the verge of defeat. The giddy spells contracted, and we gave up keeping tabs on walls and posts that could provide support in an emergency. By the time recovery was complete, the moment had come to return to Africa.

Life resumed its normal Khartoum pattern. Sweating it out in almost endless committees, offset by the joy of lecturing under a grapefruit tree in the sweet air of early morning; breakfast in the acacia forest; examining drawings; having students to supper, when Omer Agra would lovingly play his lute, Elamin Muddethir sing love songs in a sweet tenor voice and the gentle Bolis Salib would – surprisingly – contribute a martial song called *Long Live Egypt and the Sudan.*

Maybe a year after the strange illness, we dined one evening at the residence of the British Ambassador. Among the house guests there was a face I recognised – but only after a time. It was the Specialist. Pale and withdrawn, clearly he had now exchanged places with me; and in fact I found that this sick man, drawn to the Sudan by its almost-endless sunshine, had retraced in reverse our path along the Nile.

Alas, it did not bring him to recovery. Sitting beneath our orange trees only a few weeks after meeting him at the embassy, we found his obituary in the crackling pages of *The Times* overseas edition. And so, it seemed, the final word had been said in this little tale of two travellers wandering along the Nile in search of health.

But life isn't a very good artist – it has a way of adding an untidy, tardy but undeniable postscript even when 'Finis' seems to have been written with a firm hand and underlined with a flourish. And so it happened to us close on twenty years later. In the winter of 1978, our former architectural students insisted that Margaret and I should re-visit the Sudan as their guests. No one who is unfamiliar with the Sudanese flair for providing hospitality can quite conceive what such an invitation implied. Landing at five o'clock in the morning, still wearing the anoraks we had brought from the English winter, we were each presented with a closely typed document headed *Provisional Programme.* Our eyes smarting with sweat could hardly take in the list of receptions, suppers, dinners (one afloat on a paddle steamer specially chartered for *us*), the visits to mountains in the desert, fruit farms and the new National Museum. And of course there were to be tea parties.

Enough of the fabric of the National Museum had been in existence on our

*St. Anne from an 8th century fresco formerly in Faras Cathedral, N. Sudan, now in the National Museum, Khartoum*

departure from the Sudan fifteen years before to enable us instantly to recognise its massive white exterior rising by the Blue Nile, not far from the old White Nile Bridge. Amid much that is rare and beautiful, its outstanding treasures are the painted frescoes stripped in recent years from Nubian Christian churches of the eighth to eleventh centuries, which had to be submerged in carrying out the Aswan Dam project. Like all Byzantine wall paintings, they proved to be rich in pattern and colour, but we felt that some of the figures presented a touch more humanity than we had seen elsewhere.

Yet fascinating though the contents of this museum were, for us the climax of our visit came when we spotted an old acquaintance sitting in the surrounding gardens. Semna East Temple – no other! – the building that had marked the onset of my time of tribulation.

Its new situation contrasted sadly with the crag it had occupied high above the raging Nile cataract. But it had survived, which was more than could be said of its crag, its former neighbouring fortress built by the vengeful Senusret III, or the graffiti of the long-deceased Albert Tomkins. All had disappeared beneath the surface of the new inland sea.

This time we had to wait for sightseers to move before we could get into the temple. Rather self-consciously I again let my finger slip along the groove of the carving of the amphorae; and soon we identified the wall against which we had leant while eating our picnic.

'Anyway,' commented Margaret, 'you certainly look fitter than last time we came out of that place. You were well on the way – had you been Muslim – to becoming a candidate for one of those mounds with a flag-stick, or a grave with quartz pebbles and dish of water!'

'A dish of water? But you never said anything!'

'You don't have to say everything', she replied – adding with a penetrating look, ... especially to you.'

The most memorable tea party came towards the end of our stay. We sat at long tables set out in a big U shape. For two hours we talked, consuming quantities of sticky cake, iced biscuits, fresh fruit, pepsi, coffee and, yes, tea. Then as bats began to swoop overhead, we noticed that Dr. Halim Awad had risen.

In one hand he held a slim package wrapped in fine green tissue paper; with the other he picked up a microphone that so far had lain on the table. I think I was too moved to remember all he said, but I shall never forget the affection in his voice as he made the presentation to me.

Standing behind the microphone, almost exactly on the spot where my old departmental building had been, I tore away at the wrapping. What eventually came into view was a stone bas relief. There was certainly something familiar about the design ... but thoughtfully the donors had provided a description.

'This piece is given as a present in the name of all Sudanese architects to Professor John Alexander Potter, founder and former head of the Department of Architecture

*Bas relief made by Sayed Abdel Rahim Hag el Amin*

in the University of Khartoum – during his visit with Margaret to the Sudan, 30th November to 16th December 1978.

It is an exact copy of the bas relief on the sandstone entrance gate of Semna East Temple, North Sudan. The bas relief resembles the temple architect's own figure, who is considered by Sudanese to have been their earliest architect, having practised some 3,500 years ago.'

## 8 Aeroplanes are not yet among Stocked Items

To us it seemed that trees were part of the personality of Khartoum. Without them it would have been a different place, its beauties diminished, its commonplaces turned to ugliness, its streets torrid canyons of stone in temperatures that quite often rose above 100° F. But thanks to its trees in gardens, parks, the nearby *sunt* forest and, above all, the streets, Khartoum was a city of delight. In the centre, the sandy street verges were everywhere dappled with endlessly changing patterns of leaf shadow and sunlight; and, further out, pendulous branches framed a thousand enticing glimpses of pink brick dwellings couched in thickets of flowering shrubs. Moreover the balm of the trees was not confined to a season. Most species seemed to be in leaf the year round, and any that did drop foliage covered up their nakedness with alacrity.

Most of the trees in the streets were neem or banian. The neem has a single, straight, grey trunk from which branches spread widely to form an oval crown densely covered with smooth acacia-like leaves of deep green. Of the banian there could be no better description than that of Milton in *Paradise Lost*. Having pointed out that the banian is a species of fig, he goes on to say that it is

> '. . . not that kind of fruit renoun'd,
> But such as at this day to Indians known
> In Malabar or Deccan, spreads her arms,
> Branching so broad and long, that in the ground
> The bended twigs take root, and daughters grow
> About the mother tree, a pillar'd shade,
> High overreach'd, and echoing walks between.'

In these lines the poet has captured the banian's distinctive feature – the way in which its branches send down bearded, fibrous ropes which in time root themselves and grow into trunks. Unlike neems, banians have thick foliage, of dark green heart-shaped leaves, while their arcades of trunks and branches are of a rich brown colour.

Milton also mentions the natural habitat of the banian, India. Most of the trees which graced the streets of Khartoum in our time represented the mature growth of saplings imported from India in 1905, when ten thousand were planted along most of the thoroughfares, developing rapidly into fine specimens through constant irrigation.

For shorter distances walking along the tree-shaded streets was by far the pleasantest way of getting from place to place in Khartoum. The heat was made bearable by its dryness, and the ever-welcome leafy shade was enhanced at certain times of the year by honey-scented flowers of the neems whose fragrance, like a sunny day in England, seemed to generate goodwill in every passer-by.

We rapidly decided that for longer distances cycling was the perfect answer – a discovery that a minority of our colleagues had already made. The central portions of the roads were metalled and, in Khartoum, reasonably smooth; and there were no hills of any significance. Noiselessly skimming through really hot, dry air was cycling at its best. We never tired of spinning along the embankment of the Blue Nile, past the gate lodge of the Palace with its ancient metal notice requesting visitors not to sound motor horns while crossing in front of the portico of the Palace. Later we would stand at Mogran Point, where the White Nile merges with the Blue Nile. As we watched, with due reverence, the marriage of two of the world's mightiest rivers, frequently our only company was families of pelicans playing and fishing at the water's edge.

*The domed roof of the Mahdi's Tomb Chamber*

Not far from Mogran stands the steel girder bridge spanning the White Nile and leading to Omdurman, the huge mud-built city which stands a mile downstream on a slight eminence overlooking the combined Nile waters. Within it is the Mahdi's tomb, desecrated by Kitchener a few days after the Battle of Omdurman and rebuilt and decorated in a rather sickly wedding-cake manner during the final years of the Condominium. Much more interesting was the Khalifa's house a stone's throw away. It had become a museum and here, among the many relics of Mahdist times, we found one lovely period piece from the early years of Anglo-Egyptian rule – a photograph of 'the first mechanical transport vehicle to enter the Sudan ... built in 1903 for the use of His Excellency the Governor General and Sirdar, Sir Francis Reginald Wingate.'

'Now', said Margaret, 'I wouldn't mind something like that!' It was not the first time that her imagination had been fired by outlandish modes of transport. There had been, years before, something we had not only discovered but driven in the wilds of the English countryside, when we were researching for a book on building styles and methods. It was described by some astonished Lincolnshire village scoolboys as 'a van on a motor bike': in it driver and passenger sat together with the steering wheel between them, while the wind whistled in through a large aperture which housed the vehicle's one and only front wheel. So it was not without foreboding that I noted that she was making a sketch of His Excellency's vehicle, showing not only the mechanical externals but the strange seating pattern as well: the driver at the centre of gravity, with forward-facing passengers in front of him and rearward-facing ones behind – all open to the air though shaded by a substantial canopy.

Already the serpent of mechanical transport had begun to slither into our bicycle-riding Eden; but a few more weeks, a few more events, were needed before we ourselves would become aware that this had happened.

About a month after our visit to the Khalifa House museum we found ourselves in Mr. Vanian's shop in the centre of Khartoum. By the standards of the city and the time it was a large shop. But what mattered was not its size but the fact that it had 'atmosphere' – that indefinable quality that so few shops have nowadays. It was somewhat reminiscent, on a smaller scale, of the Army and Navy Stores as it used to be in London's Victoria Street: the same show cases of plate glass edged with bronze, the same potted palms marking the fringes of seas of carpets, the same sedulous attention to the wishes and whims of every customer. What was not in stock could and would be procured – though, as the customer would understand, this would take time.

Whatever Vanian's 'atmosphere' consisted of, one of its elements was a whiff of nostalgia. The piles of sun helmets and the traditional trekking gear stacked high seemed curiously alien even to the Sudan of that time. So it came as something of a surprise to be introduced by Mr. Vanian to a large Sudanese gentleman of imposing presence who was happily embarked on the first stages of buying a light aeroplane.

Having broken off to greet us and introduce us, Mr. Vanian turned again to this important item of business, and as enforced eavesdroppers we heard him say what we already guessed:

'Aeroplanes are not yet among stocked items.' His tone was regretful, but not defeatist. In a firm voice he continued '. . . kulhaja mumkin,' which suggested that everything was indeed possible, and added 'bukra, ba'adi ba'adi bukra' – tomorrow, the day after, who knows?'

'Such things take time,' Mr. Vanian added, turning to us as he spoke and skilfully conveying the impression that we were being taken into a business confidence.

The prospective purchaser of the aeroplane turned out to be a member of the Sudan's first – and so far, only – parliament from a place some two hundred miles away up the White Nile. Sayed Ali – for this was the only portion of his name that we had caught from Mr. Vanian's introduction – was delighted to meet people from the University. He was himself a graduate. And to meet the incumbent of the recently-established Chair of Architecture was a pleasure, a particular and special pleasure.

'Indeed,' he went on, his good-natured face now wreathed in smiles, 'it so happens that I shall be needing a new palace, to be built in Omdurman. You understand. Perhaps you might make sketches. If you are interested it's better we meet again.'

We said we were interested. Sayed Ali was already half-way to the door.

Our own business with Mr. Vanian was very brief, merely the valuation of an old necklace for insurance. As we walked towards the bikes, which were propped against the trunk of one of the shade trees, we pondered over our recent encounter.

'I wonder,' said Margaret, 'if you wouldn't feel a bit odd, arriving at the new palace on your bicycle.'

I had to admit I hadn't thought of our transport in that light. But there was no doubt that it would be easier to move furniture – such as a couple of armchairs we had recently bid for successfully at a sale – by car rather than by bike. Then by one of those coincidences with which our lives, and probably everyone else's, seem to be studded, within a day or two one of our colleagues told us of a chap who wanted to get rid of a car. On the spur of the moment we bought it, a third chap, a mechanical engineer, having vetted it.

When the car was delivered to us it turned out to be something of a disappointment. Scouring sandy winds had stripped almost every shred of paint from its body, the winding gear of the windows was missing and so, for the most part, were the rear door handles. This last defect soon proved to be indicative of a more deep-seated malaise: the doors had a way of flying open as we rounded corners. Our solution was simple, though it involved some loss of convenience and space: a strong wire fastened at each end to one of the rear handle stubs and tensioned firmly across the car's interior.

New cars were unobtainable and import licences rarely granted. We had little hesitation in basking in our colleagues' congratulations on our good fortune. As we had foreseen the handling of bulky purchases was enormously simplified, and the car was invaluable to whisk us to and from the Khartoum round of evening functions.

The honeymoon lasted a month. Then without warning foot and hand brakes failed as Margaret drove towards town. The roundabout in our avenue was a recent innovation. It had achieved immediate popularity as a rendezvous of the faithful. At prayer times they would meet there, form into neat lines, and prostrate themselves on the grass facing toward Mecca. Preparations for one such occasion were in train as Margaret approached the roundabout. She was not speeding, but she could not stop, so she decided on the spur of the moment to switch off the engine, sit tight and circumnavigate the island until the car came to a standstill.

'The gentlemen,' she reported, 'were very interested and helpful. It was a bit like a runaway horse, but worse, because you couldn't really *do* anything.'

Clearly we needed to go and see Ezzat Kasser. He was a typical representative of a numerous class of people who, hailing from the north-eastern sector of the Mediterranean lands, had settled permanently in the Sudan and were largely responsible for keeping its service industries going. Everything from lampshade repairs to electronics, from manufacturing ice cream to repairing and rebuilding cars, came within their province.

Like most of his kith and kin, Ezzat was hardworking. He didn't mind making himself or his clothes dirty. He would get under a car himself, not tell someone else to do it. I can see him now – a man of unusually large build, dressed invariably in sweat-soaked shirt, nominally white, with voluminous khaki shorts and sandals. He simply exuded optimism; however down in the dumps you might feel when you ran him to earth in the 'Industrial District', you left him feeling buoyant.

Ezzat's business was basically the rebuilding of cars, but he was also a very good entrepreneur, capable of doing a deal in half a dozen different languages. We weren't sure at the outset which of these skills we wanted him to exercise on our behalf, but he soon persuaded us that we should use in him both capacities. First, he would do the car up, then he would sell it. He did suggest, however, that as a first step we should paint the car, and so, beneath the nearest banian tree bordering the Sharia el Gamhuria where we lived, we applied a coat or two of deep battleship grey, before passing it into Ezzat's hands.

A few days later he announced that the car was ready. We cycled to the Industrial Estate, and as we drank coffee with him he made a phone call, explaining as he held his hand over the microphone:

'Here I speak to somebody very, very rich. He it is who wants just such a car as yours.'

So evident was his delight at the coup he was about to pull off that we never questioned *why* anyone so rich should want a car like ours. Perhaps Ezzat, with his mechanic's eye, had spotted engineering virtues that had escaped us, and perhaps it was these he was describing so volubly over the phone in an unrecognisable tongue.

The plan of campaign seemed simple. We were to drive the car home. Ezzat would look after the cash side of the transaction. He went over the ground again.

'This rich man. He will come to your house, at maybe half past two. I tell him before he comes, you paid £S275 for it.'

It seemed ungracious, in view of the trouble Ezzat was unquestionably taking to point out that he was making a mistake. We'd told him £S250. Anyway he was going on:

'Maybe he give me more than £S275. All above £S250 that I keep. Good! OK! You like that?'

We said we did. As we drove home, bikes roped on the rear, to eat and to prepare ourselves for the rich man's coming, we could almost sense the force of Ezzat's optimism speeding us on our way.

But the afternoon wore on and nobody came, though we sat strategically positioned in the front garden so as to hear any sound of a car slowing down. Minute by minute the confidence that Ezzat had inspired that morning now drained away.

When it was clearly hopeless to wait any longer, we drove the car back to Ezzat's. He was both shocked and indignant to hear how his enterprise had ended on a note of bathos. For a moment, even his faith in himself and the world at large seemed to wane a little.

'Things are not so good for selling now, especially cars . . .' Then he brightened, and the glow of confidence returned.

'But there are others,' he said with conviction. 'One could pay as much as £S125. Not bad, eh? Soon I fix it.'

And fix it he did. About a week later the phone rang. We swung on our bikes to collect the cheque: £S250, with lemoon, Ezzat chattering away excitedly.

'Are you sure', I queried, 'that you are not out of pocket?' But Ezzat hadn't heard. And I felt a light but unmistakable pressure on the side of my left foot – the one nearest to Margaret. Ezzat's phone went, and we departed – on our bikes. 'Shall we go home the long way,' suggested Margaret, '. . . by the *sunt* forest?'

As for Sayed Ali and his palace, the question of our arriving by bicycle never arose: for like the 'rich man' he never got in touch with us. It is doubtful if his palace was ever built, and doubtful, too, if he could have made use of it if it had been; for within twelve months a bloodless military coup took place which probably ended his parliamentary career.

The car gone, we once again became cyclists. By now we had all the armchairs we needed; by now, too, we saw the advantages of spending more of our evenings at home; so that on balance the changes in our life-style that followed from not having a car were ones that we could positively enjoy. Anyhow, we had no choice: in Khartoum at that time, cars were not yet among stocked items.

But we remained curious concerning His Excellency the Governor-General and Sirdar's car built for him to specification in 1903. The Mah'dia Museum picture had referred to it as an Arrol Johnston. So we wrote to the Company of Veteran Motorists, stupidly overlooking the fact that this body is not concerned with veteran vehicles. Despite our error, the Secretary was most helpful. He told us that this was the earliest of all Scottish-manufactured cars, and it had a very good reputation. Nevertheless on the copy of an advertisement that he sent us, a few lines had been added in ink:

'Her gears are bust
Her engine's rust
I cannot sell her – *though I must*'

*After our time – Representation of strife-torn globe with suggestion that Africa should seek to mediate*\*

# 9 Brotherhood of Man

The telephone rang.

'Alexander!' It was Mahdi speaking.

'... Fifteen large cinema screens have arrived in my office – and one projector. Alexander, your budget is gravely overspent.'

I quickly made my way to Mahdi's office.

There he was, this huge, handsome man, sitting behind a desk on the same scale as himself piled high with paper. Below the desk top, the view from the low armchair was of impeccably white shorts and long socks, strongly-made black knees, highly polished brown leather shoes. The superstructure visible above desk-level was an imposing one: a fine head, held high even when paper work demanded close concentration, with typically Sudanese features topped by close-cropped, curly, wiry hair of black tinged with grey round the edges; and a powerful frame clothed in a short-sleeved, open-necked shirt of hoar-frost crispness.

Although Margaret and I had known Mahdi for only quite a short time, first as acquaintance and then as friend, we were already familiar with the remarkable control he exercised over his emotions and his ability to restrain or display them at will. We

---

\* Representation designed by Sudanese artist and erected by Blue Nile to mark African Summit meeting, Khartoum July 1978.

believed we had learned to interpret the significance of certain of his facial expressions – a sudden opening wide of his eyes, or a particular way of furrowing his forehead, for instance – or of subtle variations of tone of voice that he indulged in from time to time.

The day of the 'cinema screens' he looked as solemn as a judge about to try a serious crime. His eyes were open so wide that the brown irises were fielded against their white surrounds; his brows were furrowed and his lips projected – all normally auguries of 'storms ahead.' Wasn't he over-reacting to my minor predicament? So far he'd never gone to unreasonable lengths in his pursuit of fairness and efficiency.

But he really was a great leg-puller! Suddenly, having savoured my confusion enough, he threw back his head and rocked with laughter.

'Not to worry, Alexander. . . . Here I suspect the hand of our London purchasing clerk. A stop placed after a '1' may have been taken as an Arabic '5'. Your department may do well by the mistake. The fourteen you say you do not require may be sold – profitably. Inshalla, God willing!'

Then he launched on a warm-hearted peroration prompted, I thought, by his desire to set a seal of tenderness on what he had said and to remove any suspicion that his anger had been anything other than a spoof.

'It so happens, Alexander, that a misunderstanding rather like yours took place not so long ago in the Ministry of Supply's purchasing department. In that case it was not a matter of cinema screens – for them it was fire engines! One alone was required for Khartoum. However, when that particular cargo was off-loaded at Port Sudan, what do you think? Ten fire engines were uncovered in the hold, every one of them labelled to 'The Minister'. Imagine, ten! Happily we are on the whole an adaptable people, and the Minister proved to be no exception to the rule. The machines were distributed far and wide – even Wau is the proud possessor of one such British Red Engine.'

At this there was a fresh burst of laughter – just to think of that resplendent fire engine, its great brass bell shining, in the midst of a teak forest, with not a road in sight!

Big men in important positions may be judged by how they deal with the trivial. By that test, we felt, Mahdi emerged triumphant again and again. We soon realised that this man, though he might be called Registrar and be responsible for the administration of the whole University, was no bloodless bureaucrat. His administrative expertise, built on a solid academic foundation of degrees in arts and sciences from St. Andrews, was smoothed and sweetened by his warm humanity and ever ready sense of humour. So when we realized that his work in organising Appointment Boards, at which applicants for teaching posts were interviewed, took him to London each year, and that his next visit would coincide with our home leave, we immediately began to scheme. The chance of seeing this new friend of ours in a new setting, in England – or better still in Wales – was too good to miss.

We still had our tiny Welsh cottage near Aberystwyth, and fortunately the Welsh friend who lived there while we were in Africa was taking a party of students to

France. So far, so good. Now, if Mahdi could somehow arrange one of his meetings so that he could slip away to Paddington in mid-morning. . . Word came that, barring unexpected snags, he would be glad to come.

On the appointed day, while Margaret prepared a festive meal I set out for Aberystwyth in our old Bradford van – a kind of vehicle that, alas, has passed into history. Mahdi had a right to expect something more comfortable – a car, perhaps. Something more grand – a big car, like the American and German monsters we saw quite a lot of in Khartoum. I had to admit that our Bradford was built for utility, not comfort, still less for beauty. Its ancient brown paintwork was matt surfaced, though the chrome on the radiator and headlamps was gleaming still – of pre-war quality though possibly post-war manufacture.

All the drama of the railways' great age of steam attended the arrival of the London express at Aberystwyth. For here was the terminus, the point where buffers and

*Gorsfach*

concrete stood to prevent the impatient iron horse from plunging on into the sea; here was the point where at last, after hundreds of miles and hours of travel, passengers from the metropolis emerged to find themselves in a new world of wild wastes and craggy heights. It was a scene which needed a Hitchcock to capture its atmosphere, a Betjeman to catch its nostalgically picturesque overtones, the distant pillar of steam advancing rapidly towards us, the crescendo of noise culminating in the groan of steel brake shoes fighting with steel wheels, the expiring sigh of steam as passengers burst forth on to Platform 1 from every door of the chocolate and cream coaches. But amid this multitude, no sign of Mahdi! The crowd thinned. The fireman climbed down to remove his lamps from above the scarlet buffer bar. Then just as I was preparing to come to terms with the impending sense of anti-climax, a door swung out in the very last coach. The view was clear and I was able to see the word painted on the door below the open window. Mahdi had travelled First Class.

After the initial excited exchanges we stood together in the sunshine outside the station, reunited for the first time since leaving Africa. We surveyed each other's tweed jackets and flannel trousers, a change from the lightweight shirts and shorts we had so recently worn, and I turned to open the door of the passenger seat. Mahdi gazed at the frayed green patterned carpet, laid by a previous owner in an effort, no doubt, to disguise certain shortcomings in the Bradford's flooring and undercarriage arrangements. He gave vent to a deep-throated chuckle. It was a sound that spanned the visionary gap between Aberystwyth and Khartoum. Trousers might change, but not that chuckle.

'Alexander, I see that you have the green carpet of welcome laid down for me. Green! The colour of Islam!'

Still laughing, he contorted and squeezed his body into the seat, and we talked the journey through until, approaching the cottage by the back door (the front was never as handy), we were greeted by Margaret and met by the fragrance of roasting Welsh lamb.

One afternoon a day or two later Mahdi and I walked to the old church standing high on the hill behind Aberarth, from the churchyard of which most of Cardigan Bay can be seen. The broad leaves of the grass on the banks of the lane through which we passed were bent by the lightest of breezes, so that virtually every one caught and reflected the sun's rays. We mounted the slate steps, pushing open the well-wrought gate and threaded our way between the graves until we reached the westernmost boundary of the graveyard. Here by a rough stone wall which separated the cemetery from the cliff top, was the best viewpoint. Just beyond the wall the ground fell away, not precipitously to begin with, but in a gradual slope covered with gorse now ablaze with bloom. Beyond that there was a steeper gradient, sharp enough to obscure most of the flat shelf which borders the sea. Far, far below, toy cows speckled toy fields. Luminous pools of sea water lay gleaming amongst brownish grey boulders, pebble-sized to us, deserted by the fast-retreating tide; and curving round beyond the sea-bed, the distant arm of the bay and the sky above it offered an infinitude of shades of green and blue.

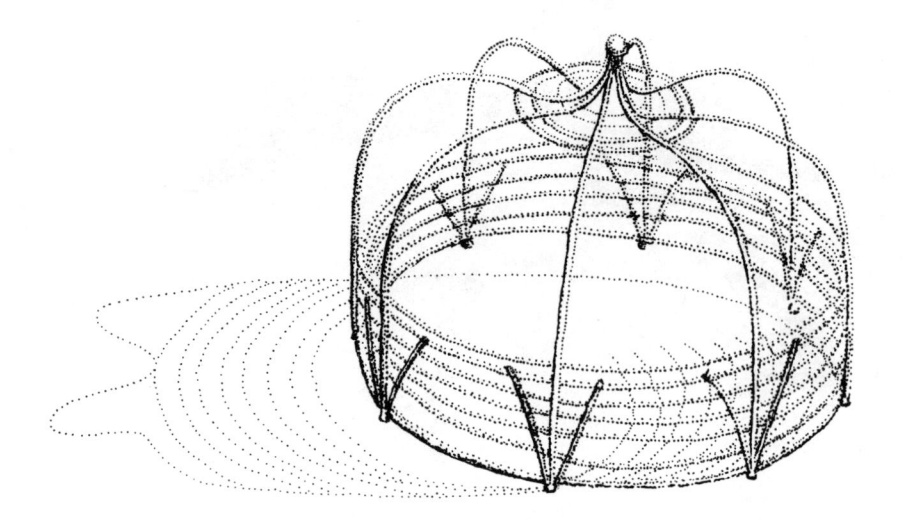

For a time we stood behind the wall, braced against the breezy air and lost in silent contemplation of what lay around us. Then we talked of building, a topic that Mahdi found of absorbing interest. We spoke of slate and how the Welsh had used it in roofs and walls. He wanted to know how the Welsh liked to plan their homes and their farms, what sort of size farm holdings were, and many other details of the interaction between land and people. So quite naturally our talk turned to the path taken by the central Welsh railway and the journey Mahdi had made from Shrewsbury across Wales to Aberystwyth.

How it popped out, I can never remember. But somehow, quite offhandedly, I made some reference to his having travelled First Class – and I wondered why he had done it. It was ill mannered of me, and it would have been unpardonable if I hadn't known Mahdi would take no offence. But it was quite a while before he answered.

'Ah,' he said, 'you noticed.'

He paused, and went on, 'For me, travelling 'First' in the U.K. is really a matter of some expediency.'

He was speaking slowly, weighing his words. His gaze was fixed on that infinitely remote region where sea and sky merged invisibly.

'By choice, providing it is comfortable and there is room, I would travel 'Third'. Meeting people interests me. I like them; you know how my house in Khartoum is usually filled with guests. Children play among the bushes. But I am a black man. And in your country, sometimes, when a black man travels 'Third', his carriage companions look on him as inferior. You can sense it!'

He could see that I was perturbed, and he hastened to reassure me.

'Oh, you get used to it. But if a black man travels 'First' he is treated in quite a different way. His colour seems to pass unnoticed. As for railway officials, this time they do not shun him. Porters compete – just think of that – to carry his luggage.'

At our feet, amid grass and weeds, funereal bric-a-brac lay littered: smashed artificial flowers, the wire cages reinforcing the domes now rusting away. My eyes wandered over the ivy leaves of thinnest metal, once silvered but now blotched with rust; I gazed unseeingly at chipped and broken pottery emblems of roses, doves and hands clasped in heavenly welcome.

What Mahdi had said had come to me like a cloudburst out of a clear sky. Till then, in my innocence I had thought of racism and colour prejudice as other peoples' problems.

There was no vindictiveness in Mahdi's voice. But he knew that I had been shocked and saddened, and that a feeling of shame made me at a loss for words.

*All-aboard for The Great Rally in Omdurman*
*(page 106)*

*Jacob Epstein: 'The Visitation' (1926). Exhibited at the 1951 Festival of Britain*

## 10 Blow, bugle, blow

> 'Blow, bugle, blow, set the wild echoes flying,
> And answer, echoes, answer, dying, dying, dying.'
>
> The Princess; a medley.
> Alfred Lord *Tennyson*

Early in life we both conceived a devotion to heroic sculpture. For that reason the open-air sculpture exhibition in Battersea remained one of our outstanding memories of the 1951 Festival of Britain; and when we got to Khartoum we were delighted to find there two splendid essays in sculpture in the grand manner – the statues of Gordon and Kitchener, the former mounted on a camel and the latter astride a charger. They were magnificent reminders of men who, in their day, played resounding parts on the stage of history. But 'Time hath an art to make dust of all things, as much of a man's reputation as his body.' Who were these men, and why were their effigies here, as large as life if not larger, enduring the blaze of Sudan suns?

Answers to the first half of that question almost lay in the realm of 'general knowledge'; and a little checking in readily accessible sources soon sharpened the somewhat misty impressions floating in our minds. Each of these men was Governor-General of the Sudan in the closing years of the last century, Gordon having two spells of office and Kitchener one – and that for only just over a year. They both found themselves in a strange and difficult position: strange because they were administering on behalf of the British government a territory which was not and never became part of the British Empire, the nominal ruler of the Sudan being the Khedive in Cairo; and difficult because they had to administer an area as great as the whole of Western Europe, plagued by unrest and having extremely scanty communications.

Nowadays Kitchener lingers in popular memory more as an ambitious leader of the Boer and Great Wars than as Governor General of the Sudan – his is the stern, mustachioed face and pointing finger of the famous recruiting poster, 'YOUR COUNTRY NEEDS YOU'. Even in the Sudan he is thought of primarily as the victor of the Battle of Omdurman, which led to his being ennobled as Kitchener of Khartoum. But in fact Gordon had closer and longer links with Khartoum, which eventually he defended for 317 days against the forces of the Mahdi until its fall and his death, in January 1885. The news sent a thrill of anguish through Victorian England; Gladstone's government was rocked to its foundations and did not long survive. This drama set the seal on a life in which Gordon found fame and honour in many parts of the world – how many other Scots have ever been designated Mandarin of China? In the Sudan, before the final débacle, he gained one reputation as an administrator, stern, paternal and fair; and another as a connoisseur of camels who was renowned for the marathon journeys he undertook.

No more than a little gentle blowing and brushing was needed to clear away the film of sand that time had deposited on these men's careers. But the story of their statues proved to be much more obscure – and in a number of ways surprising.

To begin with, we discovered that both our statues were replicas. Gordon and his camel mount were the work of E. Onslow Ford, R.A., who exhibited the sculpture for the first time at the Royal Academy Summer Exhibition of 1889, only four years after Gordon's death. Gordon was widely regarded as a national hero, and such intense feelings led easily to criticism of the statue. Why was Gordon shown riding such an outlandish beast as a camel? The sculptor replied that this was the mode of transport that the Major General had himself favoured. And any viewers of the statue with a modicum of artistic sense could not have failed to admire the way in which the camel's supercilious stance – heightened by tight reining of the beast's head by the rider's left hand – had been caught by the sculptor.

The original cast of this fine statue still stands, splendidly situated amidst lawns and trees, on the site for which it was intended in the grounds of the School of Military Engineering at Chatham. The Sudan version was cast from the same mould, and was first erected at the bottom of St. Martin's Lane, London, close by the National Portrait gallery, precisely where Nurse Cavell's monument now proclaims – as if

*Gordon depicted in his uniform of general in the Egyptian army and wearing the tarbush upon his head*

pronouncing an epitaph on Victorian imperialism – 'Patriotism is not enough.' Hardly was the mortar of the pediment set, however, when there came a change of plan – the monument was to be shipped to the Sudan and re-erected there. The first stage of the journey to Africa ended in the bed of the Thames, where the S.S. *Cedardine* deposited its cargo after a collision. In a surprisingly short time, Gordon was fished out and transferred to the S.S. *Lesbian*, which happened to be close at hand and was providentially bound for Alexandria.

From Alexandria's docks, swarming with labourers and ringing with their shouts as the cargo was transferred to the wagon of a goods train, the statue was taken by rail six hundred miles south to Shellal. The first attempt to load it there on to a steamer was unsuccessful, and the fifteen-ton mass of solid bronze rested once again for a while on a river bed – this time the Nile. Then the steamer thrashed southward, past villages built on yellow sand, glistening white against purplish mountains; past the small but massive Temple of Amada on the west bank; past countless *sakkieh* turned by melancholy buffalo to quench the thirst of the land for the Nile; past the marvel of Abu Simbel where, at a bend in the river, for some three thousand years four colossal eastward-facing figures hewn from the living rock had sat and waited for every morning's sun to flood them, and the temple which lay behind, with light and warmth.

More than eight hundred miles from Alexandria the northern boundary of the Sudan was reached; journey's end was now a mere six hundred miles away by rail, the first third of this over the stony wastes of the Nubian Desert, the remainder along the valley of the Nile. At that time the railhead was Khartoum North, on the east bank of the river, for the Blue Nile Bridge had not yet been built; so yet again the sculpture had to be loaded on board a vessel. But this time all went well.

The statue was erected – and then re-erected because Khartoum's cotton soil substratum gave way under the strain – opposite the Palace where Gordon had met his death eighteen years before. The site formed the focus of a fine piece of civic design which now began to take shape. Soon a new cathedral began to rise close by, and thousands of trees were imported to turn the newly laid-out streets into avenues.

Kitchener's statue belongs to a somewhat later period. In 1911 the Field Marshal, as he now was, was re-visiting the Sudan on an expedition to shoot big game: elephants, lions and in particular the rare white rhinoceros. The Governor-General, Sir Reginald Wingate, suggested that a statue of his distinguished guest and predecessor should be erected in Khartoum. Kitchener raised no objection; in fact he suggested that the mould used for the fine statue of him by Sydney March, which had recently been erected in Calcutta, should be used afresh.

Despite this money-saving inspiration, when Wingate came to work out the financial details, he found – it is said – that there was not enough money in the kitty to pay for all the metal, even though the Kitchener casting was to be hollow – as is usual – in contrast to Gordon's which was of solid bronze. The story goes on that Wingate solved this problem in an ingenious way: he had several tons of brass gathered up in the shape of cartridge cases spent in the Battle of Omdurman – material which was shipped to the U.K. and alloyed with tin to provide the bronze needed for the casting.

We mentioned this odd story to Sayed Thabit Hassan Thabit, the first Sudanese Commissioner for Archaeology, who for a time was responsible for looking after the statues. He laughed – a deep, throaty laugh that was characteristic of him.

'Rather insensitive to Sudanese feelings . . .?' I queried.

His reply, in a voice reminiscent of Paul Robeson, was punctuated with mirth. 'So *that* is what they did', he said, '. . . I didn't know that.'

Then he added, 'They belonged, anyway.'

And we joined in the laughter of this humane historian.

The 1914–18 war held up the despatch of the Kitchener statue to the Sudan until 1920, four years after the man himself had gone to his death in the North Sea. By now communications had changed and improved: the statue could be transported by sea from England through the Suez Canal right to Port Sudan on the Red Sea, and from there it travelled by rail, eventually crossing the girder bridge across the Blue Nile, to reach the heart of Khartoum. On its arrival a well-meaning railway official sent a message to the Civil Secretary's office saying that a parcel was awaiting collection. Accordingly a servant was despatched on his bicycle. The 'parcel' which met his astonished eyes was a huge crate containing 'Kitchener' and his steed – one and a half times life size.

Why Sydney March made the statue quite so large we couldn't discover. No doubt there are some who could claim that he was justified in making Kitchener larger than life, just as some others might have discerned a symbolic fitness in the fact that the statue was hollow; for Kitchener seems to have been a great disappointment as a wartime cabinet minister, and Arnold Bennett dismissed him as little more than 'a magnificent poster.'

Impressive though they were, both in themselves and as components for the urban scene, we had not long to enjoy them. For even at the time of our arrival in the Sudan in 1957, the statues had begun to be undermined by history. Already the Sudan's first parliamentary government under Sayed Ismail el Azhari had decreed that they should be removed. The responsibility for actually doing this, however, fell into other hands as the result of a bloodless revolution which took place in November, 1958. Margaret's diary records:

> 'Alick came back for breakfast from the University, as usual; but with a story that at midnight the army had taken over the government. I could hardly believe it! I went to the garden gate, looked up and down Sharia el Gamhoria . . . everything just the same as usual. Later we cycled through town to the Khartoum Technical Institute. The only thing that seemed out of place was a military tank parked on the grass outside the post office – a soldier fast asleep on its roof, flat on his back, knees up, his large brimmed hat pulled down over his face! A crackly BBC announcement (about tea time) said in fact there had been a revolution. When

we went to the general post office again about 5.30 pm. (opening time) the tank had gone. There were the usual crowds to buy stamps!'

On the first anniversary of this event, an article in *The Times* described our new rulers as a 'handful of gentlemen', which was probably not far from the truth. Their prime purpose was to build a nation with a common purpose from the jigsaw of races and territories that the Sudan had inherited from the period of colonial adventures. Strenuous efforts were made to foster a new spirit of national identity. A great rally attended by vast numbers of nomadic desert people was held in Omdurman. Camels in their thousands converged on the Three Towns, giving us our first chance of seeing howdahs – the 'ladies only' compartment of the camel transport world, tent-like single seaters each with its highly decorated top-knot, made to fit on the backs of the camels so as to give lady travellers complete privacy. Horsemen, too, galloped in their hundreds, brandishing ancient and beautiful weapons and wearing chain-mail armour that belonged to pre-gunfire days.

*The 'ladies only' section of the camel transport department*

Very much less exciting were the numerous foundation stone laying ceremonies which I was called upon to attend *ex officio*. And then, gently and gradually, we got wind of the fact that, as part of the process of defining and impressing the personality of the new nation, some definite action was going at last to take place concerning the two statues. This, we had come to realize, was inevitable – the only question had been when and how. Especially the latter – *how* would the Sudan carry out this act of decolonization?

The answer that was found was one, we felt, that perhaps only the Sudanese would have been capable of formulating. The 'handful of gentlemen' seem to have reasoned this way: if you can have *un*veiling ceremonies, surely you can have *veiling* ceremonies.

Our first intimation of this came as we sat under our orange trees, dividing the crackling pages of *The Times* between us in our customary fashion. One of us spotted the following item in the issue of 26 November 1958. Its dateline was Cairo the previous day.

## SUDANESE TO MOVE BRITISH STATUES

The Sudanese government have decided to remove the statues of Kitchener and Gordon from Khartoum. The statues will be kept in a museum.

Two days later, 'official quarters' were denying that Kitchener and Gordon were to be removed.

'That means they will do it,' commented Margaret, '. . . just as it would in the U.K.'

And so, thirteen days later, they did. It was a remarkable and moving occasion. An Arabic daily paper, *El Sudan El Gadid*, described it as 'a demonstration of good will . . . a proof of maturity . . . and a gesture of civilized behaviour.' In fairness, one must admit that it was all of these things. And talking after the event to some older Sudanese and British who had been present, we found that the ceremony had evoked thoughts of common endeavours in which both peoples had shared – education, the professions, cotton growing and many other fields of activity – leading to the growth of mutual respect and friendship.

The veiling of 'Gordon' began with the arrival of a guard of honour consisting of a hundred Sudanese troops who formed up facing the statue. Contrasting with their khaki-clad ranks was a band in white tunics and navy blue kilts who played a selection of Scottish airs. At half-past four precisely, the guard of honour presented arms; the British Ambassador, Sir Edwin Chapman Andrews had arrived. A silence you could feel enveloped all. A pause; and into the expectant hush a military band softly poured the opening bars of God Save the Queen, swelling magnificently to its climax as the leopard-skinned bass drummers thumped and the kettle-drummers rattled furiously on their emblazoned instruments. Buglers stepped forward, their instruments glinting fire as they raised them to sound the Retreat, its sad, sustained notes echoing round the Palace close by, where Gordon had died. Troops of the Engineering Corps slowly paid out ropes that held a tent-shaped cover suspended over the statue from a framework of scaffolding. Gently, ever so gently, it came down. The unveiling by Sir Reginald Wingate had now been reversed; after fifty-four years the wheel had come full circle. The shrouding completed, the buglers again stood forth, this time to sound the Reveille, and as their notes died away the band crashed in with the lively strains of the national anthem, *Nuba-Rigoaa*.

The ceremony was over; but it was to be repeated, for now it was 'Kitchener's' turn. Headed by the Governor of Khartoum and the British delegation, all in ceremonial white, the entire assembly moved towards the Blue Nile where the equestrian statue stood facing the Ministry of Finance. There the same military ceremony was enacted, the buglers' calls this time resounding dolefully through the massive stone arcades of the Ministry. West of Omdurman the sun was setting, flooding the white-clad figures, the troops, the neem and banian trees planted to Kitchener's orders, with its blood-red glow. There was one marvellous moment when the dying rays caught the shroud as it descended, seeming to set it on fire. Then the controlling ropes slackened;

'Kitchener' too was lost to view; hours later, at dead of night both statues were removed from their pedestals.

Though we had read in *The Times* that the statues were to be repatriated, no date had yet been fixed, nor was it even settled where they were to go. But about a month later we learned that the British government had offered 'Gordon' to the Gordon Boys' School at Woking and 'Kitchener' to the School of Military Engineering at Chatham, and that both had accepted.

Meanwhile the sculptures were hidden away in a yard behind the old Museum. But though out of sight they were not entirely out of mind. Through a friendly neighbour of ours who had connections, we learnt something that not even the Sudanese museum authorities were aware of: that the 'handful of gentlemen' caused fresh flowers to be placed from time to time before the two statues. When we asked, 'For heaven's sake why?', our friend just smiled and said, 'We understand it is a custom with you, and it is thought respect should be shown. The Sudanese respect bravery.'

There is not much else to tell. 'Gordon' arrived without incident at the highly respectable town of Woking and has settled in well amid the playing fields and mellow brickwork of the school. 'Kitchener' was rather less fortunate. Seated at ease in our garden in our favourite spot beneath the orange trees, we read in our Overseas Edition:

### KITCHENER STATUE DAMAGED

Chatham    March 7    1960

'A soldier was placed under close arrest in the guard room at Kitchener Barracks, Chatham, today after it had been discovered that the equestrian memorial of Lord Kitchener ... had been damaged during the night. The scabbard had been broken.'

## 11 Going Underground

As I sat in my office the sparrows chirping outside reminded me of England. So did the *click-clack, click-clack* of the Cromwellian clock.* From my desk I could plainly see, illuminated by the morning sun, the maker's name inscribed on its brass dial: Richard Washington, Kendall. Save for the birds and the clock, all was quiet, for it was not yet breakfast time. Soon Abdel Basit would arrive to tell me how he had got on in the United Kingdom. He was one of a group of architectural students who had been there for six months to get practical experience in architects' offices and on building sites.

More than once I had asked myself, had we really done the right thing in sending them? But they had to learn office routine and get to understand how one organises actual building work. I was looking forward to my talk with Basit: he would be able to tell me how all this was – or was not – working out in practice. As I waited I recalled gratefully how generous the British Council had been in paying for the students' subsistence, and the University in covering their fares, so as to make the experiment possible.

Had we, too, done everything we should have done for these boys before they got on the plane for London? True, they had appeared amazingly self-confident – not

---

* The 'Cromwellian Clock' is in part late 17th century – a little late for Cromwell

positively cocky, but certainly not frightened. Perhaps this was becausee, although they never bragged about it, they well knew that in a country where only a tiny proportion got to University and many children received little or no formal education, they themselves belonged to an intellectual elite.

Well, we had done what we could. We had chosen first-class-firms for students to work with, and arrangedd introductions and lodgings. We had warned the students about the cold – such cold as they had never experienced – and the frequent rain. We had tried to prepare them for the shock of living among people most of whom were coloured pink! As far as we could, we had tried to picture for them the everyday details of life in England, even down to such details as food. All of them had come for supper several times. With what I felt to be unjustified humility, Margaret had told them that what they were going to eat in England might not be as good as what she provided, but would probably be much better. And I had pointed out that if they liked what they received, they should not be afraid to ask for a second helping. 'Don't leave bits on your plate as you do here – to show that you are full. Have some more to show that you like it!' This was advice which they could – and did – act on immediately, while storing it up for use during their six months in the far country.

The Cromwellian clock made its premonitory hiccup, and a few seconds later the brass hammer struck sweetly eight times against the brass done. Almost on the instant, Basit arrived. I hadn't expected him to be so punctual, and I said something to the effect, that he was deviating from Sudanese tradition.

He laughed, eyes sparkling behind gold-rimmed glasses.

'That,' he said with a self-deprecatory wave of his right hand, '. . . is a little trick I picked up in the U.K.' I waited expectantly to find out what other newly-acquired tricks were now to be revealed.

We had sent Basit to Farmer and Dark, a large firm of architects with an extensive overseas practice, much of it in tropical countries. Basit told me how, having mounted the steps and rung the bell of their impressive offices in central London, he was promptly introduced to a Mr. David.

'Like our Daoud – the name was the same!' It seemed that this chance similarity had helped Basit to feel at home immediately.

I turned my attention to 'our Daoud', the *murasla* or messenger who at that moment was hovering around outside the open office door. With his long feather-headed wand of bamboo he was nonchalantly flicking sand and dust from the architrave of a window on to a typewriter that rested below it.

'Have a lemoon?'

Basit assented, and Daoud went off to get a couple of drinks. Through the window he could be seen ambling toward the lemoon stall, tin tray held jauntily shoulder-high on the finger and thumb-tips of his right hand.

As a senior architect, Mr. David would take responsibility for Basit. He read the letter carefully, and when he looked up he said, 'Well . . . Professor Potter thinks highly of you. We all hope you will have a very happy six months with us.'

'I said "great".' Basit was obviously going to give me his story in all the detail it deserved.

'I was full of enthusiasm. Professor, you had sent me there. I was going to plan the whole of the United Kingdom. I just came with that big spirit.'

Daoud returned. Two pint-sized glasses, each filled to the brim, stood in the centre of the tin tray, exhibiting to perfection Daoud's finger-tip control. He was smiling the happy smile of a master who performs a miracle of equipoise with consummate ease.

As Basit stirred the inch or so of sugar that lay at the bottom of the glass, his face clouded for a moment. When he took up his tale, there was a new note of diffidence in his voice.

'Mr. David introduced me to an assistant architect who was supposed to look after me. He got out some sketches and said, here was the window of a prison and would I work out the details and make construction drawings.

'Well! I really felt cross. I took the sketches and went to Mr. David a second time, and I said, "Professor Potter hasn't flown me miles and miles just to do one prison window. I am supposed to be doing design work. A large respectable scheme." I really felt insulted, and I left.'

Basit paused, and it was clear that I was expected to interject something at this stage. Rather at a loss for words, I asked if he had sought out a mosque in order to obtain spiritual guidance at this moment of crisis.

'No, indeed,' he replied. 'I was wandering in Hyde Park – wondering what it was all about. I had lost the address of Sudan House. I thought of handing myself over to the police. And it was then that I decided to go Underground!'

'*Underground*, Basit?' I had visions of a young Sudanese on the run; a victim of dubious companions; incipient vice and squalid lodgings.

'Oh, it was O.K.', said Basit, sensing my concern. '. . . under ground – the under line – underground trains.'

'Yes, of course.' I can clearly remember how relieved I felt. It must have shown in my voice.

'However long were you on the Underground?' I asked.

'Oh, most of the day. Just travelling. Once around the Circle Line takes nearly one hour, partly in tunnel, partly in open air. I kept eating chocolate until I got sick. The only thing on Underground is chocolate machines.'

Basit finished his lemoon. He had perked up considerably. It began to look as if he might have something better to say about his later stages in London. He went on:

'Just the whole day I spent on the Underground. It was fascinating seeing the people. I was standing for every lady – that you know is the tradition in the Sudan. But some of them preferred to hang on straps. I said to a man sitting next to me, who was reading a newspaper, that I thought such a choice was a bit crazy. But he didn't want to talk! That is something you do not experience in the Sudan. To me that was absolutely hilarious.'

He paused.

'Nine hours I had been on the line. And then I became additionally sick through eating chocolate. I felt terribly hungry and needed fresh air.'

'Where did your surface, Basit?'

'At Marble Arch, I think. But the geographical location is hazy. Then I remembered that I had the travellers' cheques the British Council had given me – about £30. I slept that night in a hotel. But I was unfamiliar with the money and I learnt later that I had been charged an exorbitant amount. So when I had paid the next morning it began to knock on my head that I had but little money left. So again I was wandering in Hyde Park. And there I found this elderly lady feeding pigeons. Watching the pigeons I became so hungry myself. I bought bread and cheese with the last money I had. And I too sat on a bench and I thought when I had finished eating I would hand myself over to the police. And then came this chap with a beard and sat beside me and said:

'You don't happen to be Basit?'

'And I said, "Yes, that's great. It's me! How did you know? In Omdurman people come and speak to me by name. But in London, with ten million people. . .".'

'Who was this man with a beard who found you?'

'He was a nice man. Another architect – a draughtsman. He took me back. Mr. David was very glad to see me again and he gave me a very large and respectable scheme – a whole cantonment for the British army. I swotted at it and they greatly helped and encouraged me. And when I had finished, they gave me a decent criticism of my work, too.'

'That, Basit,' I said, 'was wonderful.'

'It was,' agreed Basit. 'But listen, the best is yet to come. For afterwards I found out the entire cantonment had been designed three years ago, and was already built. But they were very, very nice about it; and they helped me to compare what I had done with the accepted scheme, and so I saw my true situation. And then I did the working drawings of the prison window. And from that I went on and worked for them very hard.'

Basit sighed. He was re-living his time in London, and I was beginning to see how worthwhile it had been. He went on:

'They really were marvellous. It was an exceptionally good office. Although you warned them not to pay me money, they were paying me money. And they bought me drawing instruments and the like. They said, "it's all right – so long as you don't mention it". And I did very much hard work; and when they found I was doing a Marina for my university design thesis, they paid for me to go down to Southampton for a couple of weeks to prepare my study.'

He paused again, and suddenly a further delightful recollection bubbled up.

'And before I left, one of the chaps in the office taught me how to swim.'

'That I can understand', I interjected. 'I guess they weren't taking any more chances. You'd given them one fright.'

Basit disregarded the frivolous remark. In fact he was miles away; and when he broke his silence it was to pass judgement on his spell abroad.

'They did exactly what you wanted them to do. They gave me just the kind of architectural experience that I was in need of.'

He smiled; and then he added something that I hadn't quite expected, something that pleased me a lot.

'And that was not all . . . perhaps I was not accepting that I knew so little and had to learn something of modesty.'

*Maria Theresa Dollar; silver mounted by Basit's father – Sayed Ahmed Awad el Karim, who presented it to the Potters as a gift*

## 12 U.F.O.

The plane landed; but the sandstorm which had hidden the ground from us while we were approaching the airstrip still raged. So it was a little while before we were able to spot Margaret Shinnie, though she was standing waiting for us in the desert not far from our landing place. It was kind of her to tear herself from the archaeological site and travel miles to meet us.

By the time we had walked through the broad streets of Wadi Halfa and reached the bank of the River Nile, all trace of the sandstorm had vanished. The sun shone from a sky of deepest, unblemished blue, and when we crossed to the west bank in the old landing craft which plied as a ferry, there was scarcely a ripple on the river.

The Shinnies' Land-rover was waiting for us on the other side, and within a few minutes of disembarking we were travelling northward in the direction of the Egyptian border. Fifteen miles or so of rolling comfortably over the hard, smooth surface of the sandy desert brought us to the untenanted village of Debeira West where we were to live for a while during February 1964.

It was a crucial moment for archaeology in the Sudan. Large areas known to be rich in relics of past civilizations would soon be submerged for ever under the impounded Nile waters when the Aswan Dam was completed. Time was all too short. UNESCO had mobilised teams of archaeologists from various parts of the world, assigning each to a particular site. Peter Shinnie, Professor of Archaeology at the University of Ghana, Legon, was the leader of a team from Ghana which included his wife, Margaret, who was also an eminent archaeologist in her own right. They were working in this remote place, some 450 miles from Khartoum as the crow flies, and we had come to give what help we could.

Soon after our arrival in Debeira we walked up a low hill not far from our house. At its summit was a very ancient pyramid which though it had lost its apex, was an impressive sight. Much of its brickwork, bonded into courses, was in such a perfect state of preservation that we could place our own hands within the impressions of fingers, thumb and palm left by brickmakers of three thousand years ago.

From the hilltop we could see the entire village and the even wider area covered by the 'dig', with the three houses occupied by the Ghana Expedition (including the nearest, which was for our sole use) in the foreground. All the villagers had departed: we had a sensation of having been transported into an ageless world beyond the confines of time or human control.

Having drunk in the scene we returned to our temporary home. It was made entirely of mud, with single-storey rooms on three sides of a central courtyard and a high screen wall on the fourth side. A bench-like structure known as a *mastaba* ran round the courtyard on the built-up sides, and on this we sat to draw. By our sides, on the mastaba, stood huge *zeer* pots of baked clay brimming with cool water; and from where we sat we could look through a jagged aperture in the screen wall, where there had probably been a door, to an unobstructed view of date palms, silt-loving green vegetation, a deep blue strip of river and – far beyond – the brown smear that we knew to be the east bank of the river.

It seldom rains in Northern Sudan. We were told that prior to his departure – reluctantly – for his new place of abode, the oldest Debeira inhabitant had raked his muddled memory before hazarding an opinion that there had been a sup or so some twenty years previously. Here, therefore, as in other parts of the lands of the Nile, there was no penetration of the earth by rain, and the warm, dry sand had provided a perfect preservative for architecture and artefacts. The absence of rain also meant that mud walls, such as those of our house, survived for many years, particularly when plastered with a mixture of donkey dung, water and sand. Roofs, however, could be of exceedingly flimsy construction. The rafters of our rooms were palm tree logs spaced at intervals of fifty centimetres or so; on these were laid palm fronds known as *gerid*.

Dark brought an end to drawing, and with it came a rapid fall in temperature. We went up steps from the courtyard into one of the rooms. One could hardly say we went indoors, for as we looked up we felt more as if we were under a tree than in a room. The *gerid* had been sadly neglected by the last occupants, no doubt because of their impending removal; and through the gaps between palm fronds moonlight streamed down and a myriad stars studded a crystal-clear sky.

We planned to have a quick wash, a change of clothes and then go to the Shinnies' for supper. Thoughtfully they had sent a couple of buckets of steaming hot water which we mixed with some from the *zeers* outide. Off came our few clothes, and

*Church at Debeira West excavation. Absence of rain penetration and a warm sand covering allowed much of the plaster covering of the apse to survive*

Margaret stepped into the large galvanised pan provided for our ablutions. The idea was to stand in it, swill feet and lower limbs, and complete the operation by each having a bucketful of water chucked over us.

A hurricane lamp stood on the earth floor in one corner of the room. The effect of its soft yellow light was delightful. . . .

'Come on, get on with it.' Margaret was ready for the bucketful, and I had the handle in my hand – not without a relish of anticipation. But at that moment, we heard a very curious buzzing noise, at first faint but rapidly growing louder. I had no doubt about it – it was making straight for us. The buzz became a roar, and it – whatever 'it' was – passed right over our tattered roof. We ducked. The sound diminished, dying away in the distance. Then it stopped. Within seconds we were in the courtyard. Nothing! No wind. No clouds. Palm trees unruffled. No night-flying birds or mammals. Moonlight and starlight, and deep shadows everywhere.

Though we couldn't imagine what had caused the noise we felt sure the Shinnies would be able to explain it. After all, Peter had been Commissioner for Archaeology for years in the Sudan, and both had worked on excavations in all kinds of remote places. They must have experienced every kind of weather phenomenon the Nile valley had to offer; they knew the people, could speak Arabic fluently and – if history held the key to any mystery – were able to translate the ancient hieroglyphs.

As soon as we arrived at their house we almost fell over each other to tell the Shinnies what had happened. They were pretty calm about it.

'Oh,' said Margaret Shinnie, 'You just heard the *whoosh*. Curious, tonight we didn't. It was completely quiet, wasn't it Peter? But we've heard it many times, all over the Sudan. And I can tell you, far out in the desert it sounds very peculiar. We thought at first it must be a flock of birds – a huge flock to make that amount of noise. But there were never any big birds about. It's a mystery – we don't know what it is at all.'

Later we learnt from our art-historian friend, Dr. Wenzel, that folklore ascribed the *whoosh* variously to Saracen horsemen tearing across the heavens in chain mail, or to the flight of large female birds descending from the sky to mate with male hyenas.

For ten years and more the phenomenon went utterly without explanation, until a day when our old friend and former student, Basit, was with me in my office at Queen's University in Belfast. Since our Khartoum days he had become increasingly intellectual in appearance. As we talked about a research project he had embarked on, his thoughtful searching eyes gazed at me from gold-rimmed spectacles anchored in a shock of black hair which radiated from his sallow face as if electrically charged, interrupting the rhythmic march of Margaret's Islamic calligraphy from end to end of the white wall behind him. Inevitably talk turned at length to the time when we had first known each other. 'One thing we had no success with', I reminisced, 'was finding an explanation for the *whoosh*,' and I went on to describe what had happened.

'You never heard tell of it?' I asked, less than half-hopefully.

'The *whoosh*. Yes, indeed – I've heard it. In Omdurman.'

I was dumbfounded. For a bit we sat in silence, save for the wail of a distant fire engine. I looked through the window at the whirling beech leaves and lichened stone.

'Oh, yes. I heard that noise – so did my mother. I didn't want to believe it at first. And yet not total disbelief. Then I tried to imitate the sound; and when I wasked what it could be, my mother answered me in a strange way:

'"*You listen but you do not see.*"

'I had heard some people talk', went on Basit, 'of a holy man, Sheikh Gharieb Allah. When my mother spoke of him she called him Sheikh Allah *el Tayar* – meaning "the one who flies"; and she told me that those who called on him in distress could expect to find comfort and salvation.

'This Sheikh was a great preacher and is regarded as a saint. He died many years ago, and I cannot be sure when; but he lives still – that is the belief of the many who are his devoted followers. He has a mosque in Omdurman, and close by a *'gubba'* – the tomb in which he is buried.' Then, as is not uncommon with the Northern Sudanese, Basit's conversation veered from its somewhat metaphysical tack to one which seemed to lie in a much more mundane and practical direction.

'As I became older I sometimes said my prayers in his mosque because I had missed the Omdurman Friday mosque. The time for prayer at Sheikh Gharieb Allah el Tayar's is about half an hour later. There I would pray among the *howareen* – his followers. But it is terribly uncomfortable, I must admit. You do not kneel on a thick carpet or closely woven *birsh* as in Omdurman, but upon a hard mat which is typical of the spirit of humility that prevails; and you are required to kneel in a disciplined and uncomfortable posture.'

Interesting though all this was, I thought we were wandering rather far from the riddle of the *whoosh*, and I determined to try to bring Basit back on course.

'If it *is* the Sheikh, why does he make so much noise about the flying, and how does he do it?'

'Nobody', explained Basit patiently, 'gives you a clear answer on how the flight is accomplished. All they say is, "Call on him in need and he will come". You are not required to understand whether he himself flies like a great bird or whether there is an image with flapping wings. Sometimes men hear the *whoosh* when they have been performing the *zikr*.'

'The zikr, Basit?' I demanded. 'What ever is that?'

'Literally it means a ceremony in which rhythmic swaying takes place in honour of God or a holy man. And as swaying continues you reach a state of religious ecstasy and the followers chant, 'la illaha illa Allah', 'la illaha illa Allah', 'la illaha illa Allah'.* The chant follows a key, just as in modern times when, say, you go to do a bit of 'transcendentalism' in London. In Omdurman the same thing happens: the Imam – the leader – sings the keynote for the others to follow.'

With lips tightly compressed Basit purposefully sounded a high note. After a moment or two his humming gave way to an energetic chant, 'hay-ghayoom, hay-ghayoom.'*

'It is supposed to aid concentration,' he added helpfully. But I gathered that he did not altogether approve of the *zikr*: as one brought up in the paths of orthodoxy, he evidently viewed it with a certain amount of suspicion, commenting 'It is more or less "physical", and to my mind a little bit hysterical.'

There was a pause, and then, 'hay-ghayoom, hay-ghayoom' . . . the chant was in full swing again.

The pulsating wails of more fire-engines were borne to us on the humid autumn air. Inconsequentially I found myself noting how their rhythmic pattern sometimes complemented but more often clashed with Basit's.

---

* 'la illaha illa Allah' means 'No God but Allah' and 'hay-ghayoom' may be translated as 'the Eternal who guards our wellbeing'.

Silence followed; Basit was reflecting. Eventually he delivered himself of his thoughts. 'I do not really mind *zikr*. It may help you to get involved in religious practices. And some people like it that way.'

It was my turn for contemplation, and I dwelt on countless examples of tolerance we had met with among the Sudanese. This, I felt, was one of the reasons why they had been such a joy to teach. . . . Then Basit's voice pierced my thoughts, its tone unaccustomedly firm and authoritarian.

'Go back to the roots of Islam.' I noticed how his usual mild, shy manner had been replaced by one of sternness. 'Islam is *not*, underline *is not*, a matter of physical performances. Its essence is personal prayers with God. The physical observances are secondary; they are additives, incentives. That is all that I can say.'

So we had found no explanation; yet in some strange way we felt that the search itself had brought a measure of enlightenment. Somehow the question of what the *whoosh* really was now seemed relatively unimportant, and we might have been content to relegate it to a pigeon-hole of our minds labelled 'Unsolved, perhaps Insoluble.' Yet when we visited the Sudan some four years later, its lure was still strong enough to cause us to seek out the mosque and gubba of Sheikh Gharieb Allah el Tayar.

To find them would have been difficult indeed without the help of our cherished friend Dr. Halim Awad. As any good friend is apt to do, he had insisted from time to time on helping us in our hour of need, painting the loftiest ceilings of our eighteenth-century home in Northern Ireland, and then years later in Blaenau Ffestiniog loading up roofing slates from a mountain quarry on a pouring wet Welsh day. We knew him first, however, as others of his colleagues in Khartoum University did, as an academic of indisputable brilliance, whose thesis on English landscape designers of the eighteenth century had won the praise of his Russian examiners when he presented it to them – and argued it – in their own language. It was the perfect subject for him; for his own conversation, like the landscapes created by Capability Brown and Humphrey Repton, was innocently laden with ulterior meanings. What precisely did he mean, for instance, when he said of his Russian professors, 'A lot of my information seemed new to them; but then, I did not omit to provide some few things concerning the "surprise view"'? Had his professors, we wondered, discerned the ever-present sense of fun that we read in the glint of his eyes and the lively play of his features? How had they reacted to his habit of allowing a sparkling stream of ideas and quips to pour from his lips, constantly surprising not only his hearers but also – so it seemed – himself? Did they realize how apt he was to leap without warning from one plane of discourse to another – a trait reminiscent of those landscape designers that he so admired, who had a way of creating sudden, disguised changes of level which they called, most appropriately, ha-ha's?

From admiration we had long since progressed to friendship; and now Halim, whom we knew by now in so many contexts as one who did nothing without doing it well, deftly guided us into the more sequestered parts of Omdurman. Great clouds of sand flew up from the wheels of his car as we crawled along unmade roads between acres of high, mud-walled houses. We dodged donkeys, crept round children at play, skirted deep ditches and ever-so-gently nosed goats and sheep out of the way. At last we could see the pointed dome of the Sheikh's gubba projecting above the flat roofs. Alongside it there rose a slender, silver painted tower which we rightly assumed to be the minaret of the Saint's mosque.

In the sandy and spotlessly clean courtyard of the mosque, we stood and gazed around as Halim engaged in lengthy conversation with the Imam and some of the *howareen*. At length Halim broke off to explain.

'They follow', he said, 'their own way of religion. We call it *'Tarikh el Suffeah'*. They beat drums and sing psalms which are probably the sayings of Sheikh Gharieb Allah el Tayar. To-night is not only the eve of the Holy Day (Friday); it is also the Muslim New Year's Day, *'el Sana el Hijnah'*.

The layout of this mosque, like that of all other mosques, followed the plan traditionally associated with the Prophet's own house, its principal feature being a courtyard with a large public room for worship on one long side built to full width.

Later that evening it would assume something of the character of a club or social centre for the faithful; and still later, said Halim, the *howareen* would perhaps take part in the *zikr*.

'The *zikr*!' I exclaimed. 'And as they do the *zikr* may they not hear the *whoosh*?'

'Well, yes. . . .' Halim was thoughtful. I could sense that he was struggling to find a way of expressing thoughts that are beyond words.

'Well, yes.' Then he continued. 'One of the Sheikhs answers your question in this way. He says; "Yes, you get these feelings while you are in the remembrance action – in the midst of your devotions."' As he said this, my mind flew back to Basit's mother's remark:

*You listen but you do not see.*

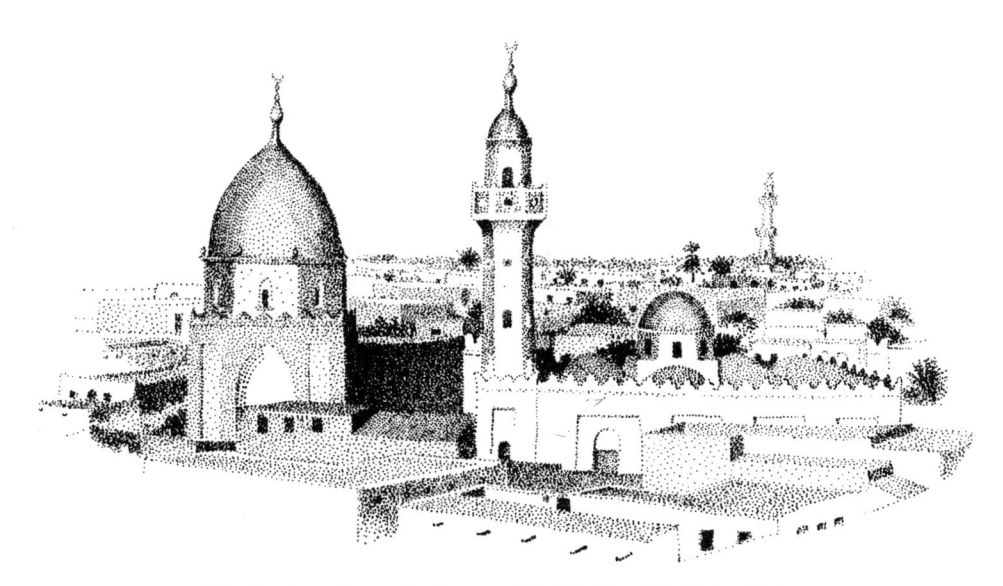

*The domed gubba and minaret of Sheikh Gharieb Allah el Tayer*

'Mmm . . .', Margaret was ruminating, 'Halim, *we* were not in the "remembrance action" when *we* heard the *whoosh*, nor were ablutions followed by *zikr*!'

'Of course!'. Halim's voice was expressive of surprise – shock even – that such rites should be thought of as essential preliminaries to manifestations of the supernatural.

'Every child is born Muslim by nature', he announced, '. . . and each will be judged by his intentions.' Then, seemingly as much to his astonishment as ours, he popped out with:

'You could say Margaret's onion soups have a connection!'

Reeling from the shock of this remark, we gradually came to see that Halim was calling to mind a kaleidoscope of memories of our former Khartoum home where – much to the delight of successive parties of students who visited us – onion soup was a favourite item on the supper-time menu.

'We were a family, eating, laughing, working together – sharing. A community. We, in the Sudan, love that. Why should any of a sharing community be deprived of the miracles of saintly men?'

Question was being answered by question, and I followed suit, continuing our discussion as we sat in Halim's car in the shade of the precinctual wall. 'The men we have just been talking to – where do they stand in the hierarchy of the mosque? Are they in any sense high officials?'

'Not officials,' Halim replied 'but rather students, pupils of the Sheikh Gharieb Allah el Tayar. They probably came here as children and will pass their days here as devotees of the Sheikh Gharieb Allah el Tayar who is buried under that gubba. Their lives are dedicated to the cause of Islam, which was his cause.'

Instinctively we turned, all three, toward the mosque. On the topmost extremity of the dome of the tomb, affixed to its delicate finial, the gilded crescent of Islam glinted and glowed in the declining sun, against a background enriched every moment by deeper shades of purple.

Halim glanced from the mosque, his brown eyes looking straight ahead and narrowing a little as he said slowly in measured tones, 'It is just a matter you hear. Far better not to scrutinize and analyse for material explanation. A brightening of the light, the movement of a white cloth, the *whoosh*. These things *do* happen. It is true.'

*The dome of the Sheikh's gubba*

*A country gubba*

## 13 Tell me, Grandfather

Poring over our maps gave us a foretaste of the expedition we were planning and a glimpse of some of its hazards. Unlike our tents and sleeping bags, which had to be ordered from England, these maps were readily available on the spot from Khartoum Survey Office. Printed in fine black line direct on to white linen and prominently lettered 'Anglo-Egyptian Sudan' with the date 1933, these maps recalled a vanished age. But what was a mere twenty-five years in a land that had changed little since its volcanoes died, leaving vast areas littered with mountain-carcases, whose forms were faithfully recorded in the vignettes which adorned the maps? Decorative as they were, however, these stamp-sized sketches of mountain features had a serious intent – to guide any unfortunate traveller lost in the desert, a fate of which the maps contained other reminders. The tracks of some wayfarers were indicated by dotted lines with names and dates, mostly ending, as they began, in some inhabited place, or occasionally shooting off the edges of the sheet to what one could reasonably hope were satisfactory destinations. But there were some which dithered to extinction in areas of white linen. It did not escape our attention that one of these concluded with the epitaph 'No water. 1912'; and frequently the maps had no more information to give about a vast tract of territory than a single discouraging word: 'Unsurveyed', or 'Uninhabited', or 'Waterless'.

To take a party of fifteen students into some of the barren areas covered by these maps was, clearly enough, no light undertaking. But it seemed an essential part of their education – and our own – that we should visit and study some of the fine ancient buildings that were to be seen in Northern Sudan.

Railways and buses – popular among the Sudanese – did not penetrate the country we hoped to visit and roads were non existent. Therefore we decided to travel by truck, though we knew that even the rugged vehicles available from the Ministry of Works had sometimes found the going too tough for them.

In addition to the students and ourselves there was Ann Graham, an English geographer doing post-graduate work at Khartoum University, who was to be our navigator. The university lent us three cooks, while from the Department we took our *murasler*, the faithful Daoud. Altogether, including the drivers of the two trucks, our party numbered twenty-four.

After our study of the maps, it was no surprise to see how carefully Margaret checked the waterbags as we loaded up. At the least sign of a leak, they were replaced by a sound one; and then, securely stoppered, they were firmly lashed to the sides of each truck. In the first few days of our expedition, Ann reported from the leading truck that she had had many a good-natured argument with the driver, Disougi el Amin, about the position of water-holes. She sounded cheerful and relaxed about it all, but we were relieved to find that between the two of them they never failed to locate whatever water-hole we were aiming for as our next camp site.

Almost as soon as we left the outskirts of Omdurman behind us, we found ourselves in poor savannah country. Dried, scorched, yellow grasses stretched to apparent infinity, waist high, to the south-west, looking for all the world like a neglected wind-battered English cornfield when the summer sun shines low upon it. On our right rose a rocky hill – Jebel Merkhiyat, on the far side of which the Battle of Omdurman, so vividly described by Sir Winston Churchill in his book *The River War*, had taken place.

When the savannah ended it was gradually replaced by undulating stony ground, broken occasionally by scattered ridges. In this unpeopled and trackless region it was astonishing to come across a wooden hut with an ancient fascia board on which we read in faded Arabic calligraphy the legend 'Gahwa Omer Hassan' (Omer Hassan's coffee house). Who were the prospective customers? How could they have come there? It was the most striking example we had ever seen of the unbounded optimism of the small business man.

Our first day's journey ended in a shallow depression called Wadi Muqaddam. Here there was a plentiful supply of water, drawn from deep wells, for the nomadic people living there at the time and for their animals. Shrubs and small plants were able to survive, but as one stood in this oasis and looked outward in any direction the land stretched flat, stony and treeless to the farthest horizons.

A further day of driving across the now familiar undulating plain of stones and sand brought us to an area where the individual colours of rock, gravel and sand merged to produce a hue reminiscent of the prunus leaf. Then in late afternoon we pitched our camp in an awe-inspiring desert region, where the unvarying flatness was relieved only by a hint of low hills far off and barely visible in the fading light, and where the reign of stillness and solitude was absolute. Water consumption had been higher than anticipated, thanks to the enthusiasm with which our students had splashed about in their ablutions before prayer the previous evening, and Margaret Water-Authority felt the moment had come for a short homily.

'Try sand,' she said. 'In Europe we used it sometimes after a long day on our tandem bicycle. It cleans even the dirtiest saucepans,' she added encouragingly.

She stopped to give a demonstration. It was, to tell the truth, more a 'lick and a promise' than a wash, more a dry clean than a ceremonial ablution. Not that there was any lack of sand: it lay about us in every direction, but Margaret was noticeably choosy about what she picked up to perform the cleansing action. Wide-eyed and open-mouthed, the students stood mutely observing this unusual spectacle.

It was already cool, and as night came on the air became bitterly cold. Hassan Yassin Bedawi, the most devout of the students, was content to use the merest trickle of water for his ablutions before committing himself to Allah's safe-keeping through the night ahead. In their tents our students, unaccustomed to low temperatures, heaped blanket upon blanket and then raided the trucks for any scrap of material that might give them extra cover.

The next day one of the students, Mohammed Mamoud Hamdi told us how the cold had kept them wakeful and talkative. 'We talked a great deal about the doctrinal rights and wrongs of substituting sand for water in the purification act. We also talked about the girls.' It had not escaped their notice that Ann preferred to sleep outside under the stars, rather than in the tent.

'And what did you make of the girls?' I asked.

'We thought they are plucky and Ann is too brave for a girl,' said Hamdi.

When the dawn came, it was a great orange glow against which the remote hills now stood sharply silhouetted in black. First out was Hassan Yassin Bedawi, to make his obeisance towards Mecca; then one by one the others, each taking strength from the example of his predecessor like the birds in a British dawn chorus; and soon we were enjoying the mighty breakfast that our cooks, Suliman, Salih and Mohammed, prepared for us.

The further north we went, the more the proportion of loose sand increased. Shoving, digging and revving the lorry engines occupied as much time as actually moving forward. And though Disougi and the other driver, Adam Mohammed Bushara, displayed great skill in picking the best routes through this treacherous terrain, the combined strength of the whole party was often needed to get us out of the stickiest spots.

We struck the Nile in the vicinity of a little place known – to the mapmakers – as Ed Debba. By now the great river had grown tired of wandering from east to west and had recommenced its northward flow toward the Mediterranean – a distance of 1000 miles in a straight line, but much further off in river-miles. The villages strung out along the Nile in this area were rich in architectural interest. We found, for instance, markets where white-painted piers supported great timber-beam roofs; there were *gubbas* of clay, brick or mud, some of them having a curious rib construction; and the minarets of the mosques displayed a rich variety of forms. In this neighbourhood, too, was the church of Dongola el Aguz, perched on an isolated crag from which its own, massive, battered walls seemed to have been extruded some twelve centuries ago.

We were making our first contact with the buildings we had come to see, and with some we had not expected to find. Our students were getting obvious pleasure from making drawings to record their discoveries. The glare of white paper in brilliant sunshine, the discomfort of squatting on one knee, and the marring of drawings by dirty sand marks – all such minor difficulties were brushed aside with a laugh. A collective decision soon emerged to hold a Great Exhibition of drawings when we returned to Khartoum.

In one place we found 'locals' wearing, somewhat ominously, a kind of stocking mask covering their heads and upper necks in a fine mesh through which their features were indistinguishable. Many of them increased the awesomeness of their appearance by dying this curious headgear with red or green pigment. We soon realised why they dressed in this way, when our party was attacked by a plague of

*A* gubba *of clay, with ribbed roof construction*

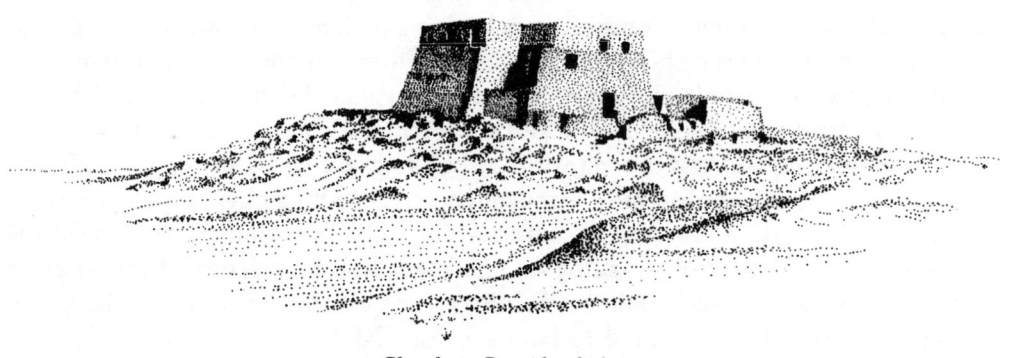

*Church at Dongola el Aguz*

flying insects. Clouds filled the heavens as eyes, noses, mouths and ears began to silt up. The purpose of the masks was now clear, and a supply of these sensible items was soon acquired for all the members of our party. Wearing the masks protected us from the pests but it also impeded our hearing and made it often impossible to guess to

*Students sketching a mud-built mosque*

whom we were talking; and tropical landscapes took on a new and alarming intensity when seen 'through the veil'. But otherwise problems were few once we had mastered the art of raising the mask at the front for each mouthful when we were eating.

One site we had earmarked for a camp lay at the foot of the spectacular Nuri pyramids. We arrived at night-fall when the huge shapes of the pyramids stood blackly against a sky from which daylight had almost been banished by a majestic full moon, just starting on its processional way through crowds of stars which glowed already with an intensity city dwellers can hardly imagine. About us and doubtless beneath us lay the relics of Sudan's most ancient capital city Napata, from which African kings of the Sudan had ruled Nubia and all Egypt some seven centuries before Christ. The ancient hub of empire was now an empty desert; metropolis had become a huge necropolis; and this thought so worked on the imagination of our highly-strung *murasler*, Daoud, that his fears of ghostly apparitions had to be quietened by a heavy dose of 'Aspro', which the students apparently carried with them in large quantities. Only then could ablutions be resumed, and peace restored to our weary party.

By now we were well accustomed to a 'trick' that the Sudanese loved to carry out. In principle, it consists of performing an impossible service, without being asked, at incredible speed. In practice it can take a thousand forms according to circumstances. A particularly endearing manifestation of this national characteristic was provided by the local representative of the government in the Napata region, Sayed Abdullahi Hassan. We came upon him without a word of warning; he laughed off our apologies but in no time opened up the little museum of Merowe for us, and in next to no time he produced, seemingly from nowhere, a river craft which he claimed to be large enough to take the smaller of the two lorries. Any idea that we might sink his boat produced great bursts of laughter. His species of schoolboy humour matched mine; soon the infection spread to the rest of our party and we were answering guffaw with guffaw. Fortunately there was little question of danger: any disaster, if it had come,

*In the underground chamber of Zuma*

would probably have happened before we got into deep water. But all went well: Disougi did his normal faultless job in driving delicately on board – fortunately by then he had been able to dispense with his mask – and we made our way safely to the eastern bank of the Nile.

We had a particular reason for wanting to cross the river at this point, for here on the eastern bank rises the holy mountain of Jebel Barkal, about which there is a group of pyramids, toppled temple masonry and carved stone slabs. Like bumble-bees invading broad-bean blossoms in an English spring, our students swarmed over these slabs to make rubbings of the designs. Then, only a short distance away, at Zuma, we descended into underground chambers where we gazed by the light of sputtering candles at the coloured wall pictures of ancient white-shrouded Sudanese kings who, heads erect and bellies downwards, rested in eternal discomfort on couches of vaguely Regency pattern.

When we pitched camp near Jebel Barkal, a certain tension pricked through our tiredness. Not only was there the ever-present threat of scorpions, but a menace of an unfamiliar kind – an invasion of snakes, small and brown, difficult to distinguish against the sand and – we had been assured by the people in the nearest village – very vicious. They had to be, because they were the guardians of the treasures lying buried in the tombs. For good measure there was a graveyard nearby, but that night Daoud was not the only one, I fancy, who took a dose of 'Aspro'.

Some 250 miles south-west of Napata and Merowe there is another area, in the vicinity of Shendi, where there are splendid old buildings. This was our next objective; and to reach it we had to re-cross the Nile and strike out over the desert.

We by-passed the old church and monastery of el Ghazali, which is of more interest to archaeologists than to architects; and then as the sun approached its zenith, a speck appeared on the horizon ahead of us. As we drew closer we could see that it was a man on a camel; and as soon as we met, the man overflowed with pent-up talk, telling us of agonising pain that he was experiencing in his back, shoulders and arms. Instinctively he turned to Mohammed Mamoud Hamdi, taking him to be the one in charge of pills. But it was Margaret Witch-Doctor who responded to his misery. She fished out a large, round tin which had been familiar to me since early childhood. Originally it had belonged to Ma Potter; and when she passed it on to me, on the disbandment of the old home, she accompanied it with a stern rubric: 'Use it, but remember it's strong stuff. Use it in dire emergency!' I doubt if the lid had ever been taken off since the closing stages of the 1914–18 war. At that time we lived opposite the recruiting office, and Ma Potter used her medicament to soothe the pain of arthritic recruits who were then being enlisted and thrust into uniform. She claimed that it was one hundred per cent successful! From me the tin had passed into the care of Margaret, who never throws anything away; and now, here it was, being pulled out of her rucksack into the noonday sun of the Nubian desert.

The man on the camel was swaying – perhaps in the throes of an attack. The sight fairly moved Margaret's gentle heart. She held out the entire tin. It dawned on me then that the moment of 'dire emergency' had come.

'But tell him to rub it in – where it hurts!'

Then we all set off, once again on our route to Shendi and Atbara. The cameldriver disappeared amidst a shimmering heat haze which was suspended over a sea of crystalline rock.

Margaret had been sitting thoughtfully. 'I suppose', she said, addressing Hamdi, 'you were able to make it quite clear to him that he had to RUB that stuff on him, NOT eat it!' The reply was far from reassuring.

'These country people – it is difficult to understand their language. They are eating everything they find as medicine. Whatever they find, they just eat it, you know. I don't know why they all think I am a doctor.' There was a pause, and then he added, 'This is one of my problems.'

'But that's terrible!' Margaret flushed with distress and compassion. Only the fact that Ann and her lorry were by now a full quarter of a mile ahead prevented us from setting off in pursuit of the camel-man and perhaps losing ourselves amid the extinct volcanoes which, according to our maps, abounded in that part of the world.

It was Christmas Eve when we rolled into Atbara where we put up at the local school and were able, for the first time since leaving Khartoum, to have a real wash. Next morning at Christmas breakfast the boys gave us home-made Christmas cards. Margaret's was entitled 'Camping near Nuri Pyramids'. It was a pencil sketch depicting a scene of chaos: lorry, packing cases, students wearing top-coats, plates, dishes, and Margaret herself, easily recognisable because of her curly top-knot, sitting calm and serene in the midst of the muddle. Mine was of an initiation rite in which black, white and brown youngsters were being dipped rather like sheep in Britain, emerging a uniform coffee colour little removed from thet of the majority of Sudanese. The message was clear and unforgettable.

The drivers, the cooks and we three English were the students' guests for supper that night. The sight that met our eyes when they asked us in to the big schoolroom was fantastic. By a lightning process of deduction we divined that a massive green-painted table, of which now only the lowest parts of the legs could be seen, had been smothered by a pure-white cloth which in its turn had been almost totally obscured by a vast array of dishes – meats, fishes, vegetables, breads and cakes. The students had bought all the food in the market at Atbara and had cooked it themselves, from the main dishes down to the many bowls on a side-table containing sauces that were as piquant as they were impossible to identify.

And there were presents, too. For Margaret a purse made by Atbara ladies, called a *mahfeeza*, worn suspended by a cord from the neck; and for me there was a perky little orange cap, a *taqia*, which the Sudanese wear inside their white turban or *imma*. This headgear is a favourite of mine, though it is proscribed by Margaret for day to day use in Aberystwyth!

'We went all over the market, looking . . .' said one of the students, 'because we couldn't find anything to buy you.'

We knew the feeling.

After Atbara we stayed pretty close to the Nile as we headed south towards Khartoum. The countryside along the river bank was in strong contrast to the wilderness in which we had spent so much of our time. Fields of growing maize fringed the Nile; beyond these we saw many goats amid the acacia trees, the lower branches of which were nibbled by them and the upper parts by camels so that the trees assumed a uniform mushroom shape. Lacy minarets of purest white bored into the unfathomably blue sky, and round them clustered clean, mud-built dwellings which looked, and in fact were, outgrowths of the landscape itself. At the heart of these little communities there was almost always a selection of stalls selling bananas – green but ripe – glasses of tea and coffee, guavas, and sticks of sugar cane for sucking.

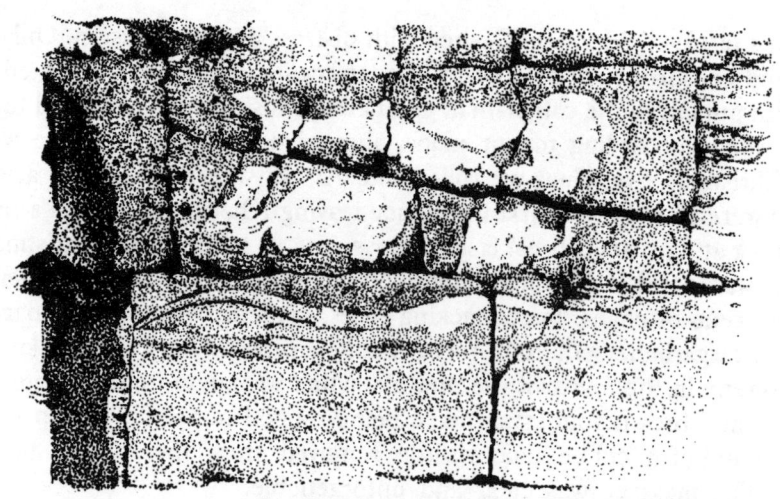

*Sun Temple, Ancient Merowe*

By way of Shendi Town we came to the area where some of the finest antiquities of the Sudan are to be found. In Ancient Meroe, the Sudan's equivalent of Pompei or Leptis Magna we discovered an affecting reminder of the petty barbarities of ancient warfare – a dado at the Sun Temple showing the cruelties meeted out to prisoners of war. Climbing up stony slopes, away from the margin of the Nile, we passed a line of some fifty pyramids, some of them in near-perfect condition, strung out along the rim

*Naqa*

of the plateau. From this eminence, surrounded by purple boulders scattered at random as if by a tribe of playful giants, we gazed at the plain which unfolded itself endlessly below, its only sign of life a camel train wending its way eastwards to the Red Sea or to the edge of the earth. No great distance away, at Naqa, we came upon Roman and Egyptian-style temples, and discovered an avenue of carved stone rams, sleeping away the neglectful centuries, without shepherd or sustenance amid the burning sands.

*Pyramids in the hills above Ancient Merowe*

*Temples at Naqa*

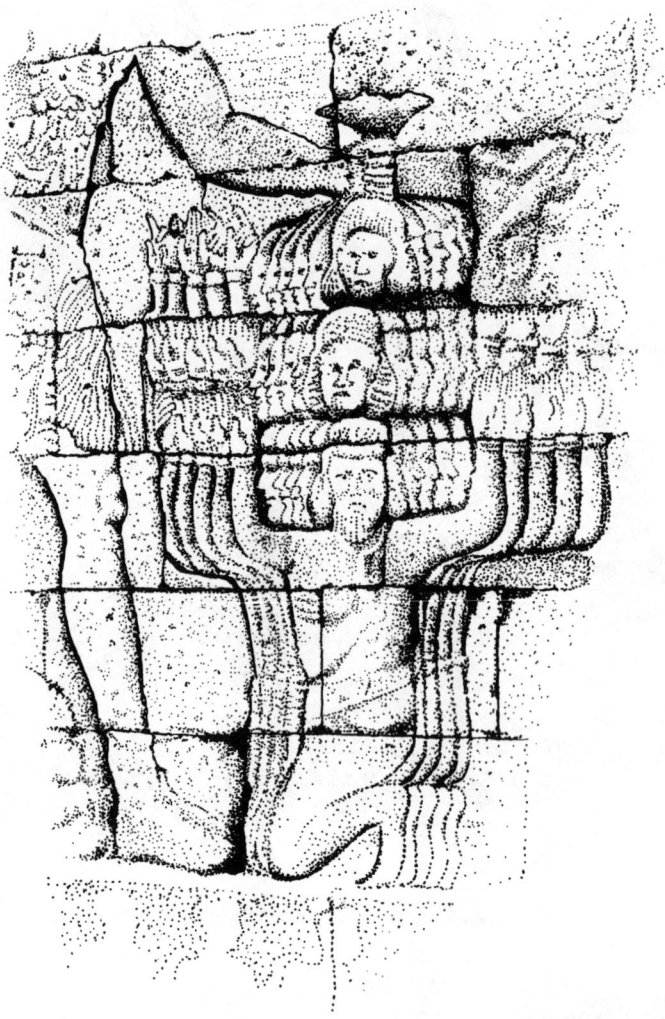

Hassan Yassin Bedawi was fascinated by a carving incised on the masonry walls of a pylon tower of the Nilotic temple. It was yet another celebration of conquest, symbolised by the cold-blooded massacring of prisoners of war. Yet at that moment it was not the still-poignant message of triumphant cruelty that riveted Hassan's attention, so much as the remarkable pattern the artist had created in depicting a stout and queenly lady administering the *coup de grace* to a batch of captives – a subject treated in similar style, but with a male executioner, on the counterpart of this pylon. 'It's most imaginative,' he murmured as he busily sketched '... no *tobe* (the present-day dress of the Sudanese ladies) on that one.'

A few more nights in camp, and of driving by day across desert wastes increasingly criss-crossed by wheel tracks and peopled by figures on donkeys and camels, brought us back home one siesta time; and we rumbled across the Blue Nile bridge as all Khartoum dozed.

Seventeen years later, almost to the day, we sat talking with Mohammed Mamoud Hamdi – that same Hamdi who had handed Ma Potter's salve to the camel driver. By now he had become a busy and well respected architect in Khartoum with – surprisingly – a summer house located in Luton. 'Under his belt', as architects are wont to say, he already had mosques and an entire complex of university buildings for a site in the south of the Sudan. The somnolent mid-afternoon silence of Khartoum, punctuated only by the tapping of a mallet on timber somewhere in the distance, provided a blank screen on to which, irresistibly, we projected memories of our trek into the desert; and soon we were laughing afresh at the substitution of ablutionary sand for water and the description of Ann Graham as 'too brave for a girl.'

Our laughter died; the springs of recollection faltered; the mallet tapped remorselessly on, transforming the lull into a silence; and then, slowly at first but with gathering speed, Hamdi unburdened himself.

'You know, it was so beautiful. The Pyramids at Nuri – I remember running during the night to see them, and then going there again in the morning. And later, when we camped near those pyramids, how wonderful it was to see the sun rise behind them, with the rays touching all the ripples of sand.'

It was deeply satisfying to hear these sentences come tumbling out. Hamdi had discovered something of beauty during that excursion. Something had wakened in him, and it was still green and fresh in his mind. That, very largely, had been the object of the tour. I felt I could wish for nothing better; but there was something he wanted to add.

'I think that for all those students who took part, it was a very fine thing for them to see that some people in the past had wanted to do work of superb quality. We respected our country all the more when we saw our forerunners had cared for it and enriched it. It helped to create a spirit amongst us, of pride and confidence. It was a morale booster! And you know it was such a memorable journey. We were a family – we caught enthusiasms and knowledge from each other, we discovered together. It is difficult for such things to pass to the young otherwise, particularly where people are drawn from nomadic backgrounds and don't have much chance of seeing buildings before they come to university.'

From one so little given to philosophising as Hamdi, this was an impressive tribute to the effectiveness of our tour; but before long he was expressing his ideas in characteristically concrete terms.

'We are now using many of the old design 'motifs' some of which we recorded on that tour. They are so beautiful, you know, and so fresh! – the fruits of many cultures. We make use of the clear colours that we saw in the ancient tomb paintings; we are aware of the decorative potential of the various calligraphies. These ideas have spread, and I think some kind of special character is emerging.'

My mind flew to Hamdi's own buildings, particularly the great mosque* of El Nilein rising at the confluence of the Blue and White Niles.

'Perhaps', I said, 'a national identity.' And he agreed.

As a busy and respected practitioner, Hamdi regards it as part of his duty to accept students for practical training in his Khartoum office. When we heard that arrangements had been made for one of them, El Hadi Yousif Ali, to spend six months in the U.K. to widen his experience we asked him to spend a few days with us in central Wales. And come he did.

It came as something of a surprise to find that he had decided to address me as 'grandfather'.

'You helped' – he explained – 'to bring understanding of architecture to Hamdi, who is now a great and good architect whose office I now attend to receive instruction. Hamdi is your 'son', for it was from you he learned many things. And now, in his turn, Hamdi teaches me, and from him gradually I too am learning. You, therefore, are my grandfather.'

'Wonderful,' I said. I could not dispute his logic, nor did I want to try, for fear of spoiling one of the happiest moments in forty years' architectural teaching.

During his stay with us we went to St. David's Cathedral, nestling in the leafy hollow which shelters it a little from the gales which scour the Pembrokeshire landscape. Its situation and external appearance delighted him; and once inside, we sat down in order to take in to the full its fifteenth century ceiling of Irish oak.

Our chairs were at the edge of a gangway running north-south along which a party of elderly ladies was being shepherded by one of the clergy. Their clothes – home

---

* The Mosque of El Nilein: designed in collaboration with Sayed Gamar Adwla, who prepared the initial designs.

made but good – suggested they might be village folk. As they halted beside us, a good many curious glances fell upon El Hadi, resplendent in pure white *gellabiya* and matching turban. The clergyman concluded his commentary on the building, and in the momentary ensuing silence El Hadi pointed to the roof. 'Tell me, grandfather,' he said, 'What do you make of those large wooden pendants hanging so fearfully overhead?'

I was aware of twenty pairs of eyes trained upon me, of twenty pairs of ears straining to hear whatever word I might utter.

'Good question – grandson,' I said.

The ladies moved on. I wasn't sure if El Hadi had twigged the questions buzzing in the brains of most of them But in a moment he turned to me, laughing.

'Pity! Had you been wearing your *taqia* perched on your head – oh, that would have been good!'

146                                  *Everything is Possible*

## 14 Suakin Besieged

Suakin was a ghost-town – that we knew before ever we set foot there; but it was only through experience that we came to realise some of the implications of the term.

This ancient port was a natural place for us to visit during out first few months in the Sudan, when we were trying to get to see as much as we could of the country and its buildings. Situated on a small island off the Red Sea coast of the Sudan, and surrounded by coral lagoons which gave it safe anchorage, in its day it had been a busy entrepôt and the main embarkation point for African Muslims intending to cross the 200 miles of sea which separates the Sudan from the holy places of Islam.

But its day had gone. If you searched for it on a map you would find its name, if at all, only with a magnifying glass. The shallow waters of Port Suakin's lagoons could not cope with the ocean-going vessels of even late-Victorian times; and Port Sudan, founded only in the first decade of the twentieth century, quickly captured all its trade. By the time we went there, to the best of our knowledge, Suakin was completely deserted. Even the sea-going pilgrims venturing on the traditional route to Mecca now sailed, it appeared, from the small mainland town of El Geyf which was linked to Suakin by a causeway built by General Gordon.

Our friends in Khartoum had promised us a feast of architectural beauties. We were warned that much was ruinous, but assured that a great deal also remained more or less intact. Another warning concerned ghosts: we gathered that as the living population had moved out, the ghosts had moved in.

Abdel Basit scorned such tales 'I hear a lot of ghost stories,' he said, in his off-hand, sing-song manner of speech, 'but I don't listen to them. I shut them off, I'm not much of a ghost believer.'

Our future Ph.D. was then, as always, distrustful of anything smacking of superstition. He had nonetheless an odd story of his own to tell of how something barely believable had turned out to be incontrovertible fact. At the age of eighteen or nineteen, he had gone with a cousin of the same age to a deserted part of the Port Sudan seafront where there was a solitary cafe, a few street lights and little else.

'In Omdurman I heard a strange thing about this part of the coast', he announced to his cousin, 'that cats walk out of the sea. Black cats. That is something I don't believe; for cats live on land.' Basit had spoken. But before long the two boys saw numbers of black cats walking through the shallows of the incoming tide, into which they had ventured to snap up a splendid haul of shellfish. 'Something interesting,' said Basit flatly, in his customary self-dreprecating way; but we assured him that on the contrary it was quite astonishing, and that in Suakin we would keep our eyes skinned for this or any other such phenomena.

The university had arranged for Margaret and me to stay in the Muhafaza, a sizeable building mostly dating from 1886, which had been first of all the residence and administrative offices of the governor of the island and then a rest-house during the period of the Anglo-Egyptian Condominium. Although showing signs of decay, the structure was still more or less intact when we were there, some twenty five years ago. It was beautifully situated, for it overlooked the ancient anchorage from which dhows crammed with pilgrims used to set sail for Jiddah across the deep blue waters of the mis-named Red Sea.

The arrangements made by the university for our stay could not have been better. Water came from the mainland in panniers slung across a donkey's back. Along the causeway too, came our cook who prepared breakfast and supper for us and then, having cleared up the supper things, departed by the way he had come. From then until the next morning we had the whole island to ourselves – in a manner of speaking.

It was dark when we set out for our first 'walkabout', though a full moon made it almost as light as day. From the market-place in the centre, alleys and streets radiated, apparently clothing the whole island with houses and other buildings. The jetties and piers which had once covered much of the island's perimeter had mostly crumbled into the water. From their remains we peered into lagoons, marvelling at the clarity with which we could see through the water to the corals below, smudged with many moving shadows that suggested the presence of fish.

The town itself was built almost entirely of coral dredged from the sea and roughly cut to cube shapes prior to building into courses to form walls. These rows of coral stone were interspersed every four or five feet of their height by round shaped logs, running horizontally and visible on the wall surfaces – a simple but effective means of reinforcing the masonry and aligning the work during construction. Nevertheless such walls, unless they are kept plastered, or at least frequently limewashed, do not last very long. So after more than a quarter of a century of neglect the whole town was steadily crumbling, and piles of débris almost blocked some of the lanes down which we ventured.

Roshans

Ruins of decorative wall niches

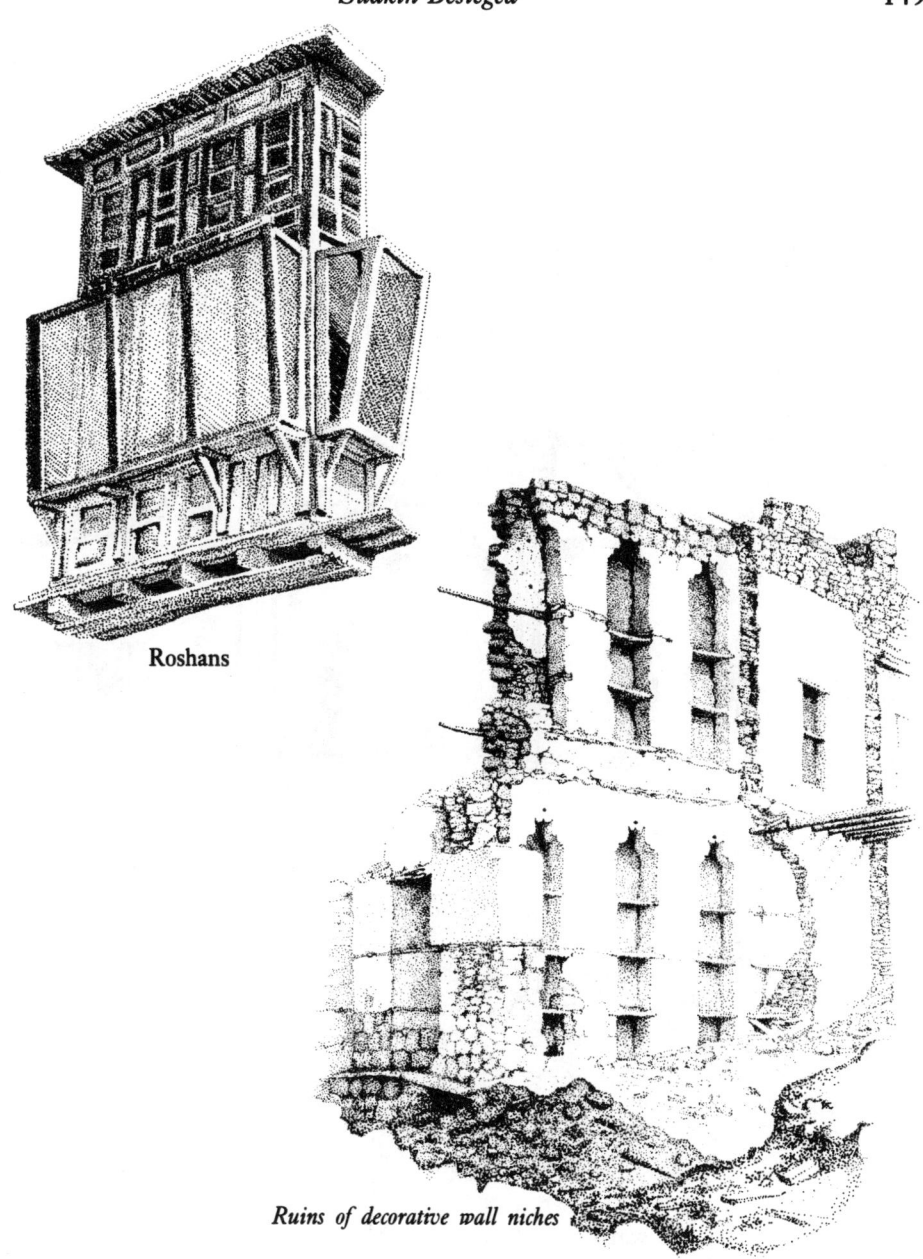

Many houses possessed richly carved wooden *roshans*, unglazed shuttered bay windows, sometimes with richly fretted shade-hoods, from which the ladies had been able to look out on Suakin's bustling multitudes without themselves being seen. Turkish influence was obvious in many buildings, notably in the doorways, with their lintels of solid stone cut into the form of a four-centred arch; and in the decorative wall niches that we could see in rooms from which external walls had fallen away.

As we turned back towards the Muhafaza, Margaret said, 'I hope we see some of those mysterious black cats.' No sooner had she spoken than we came upon a fishing party. Admittedly it was smaller than Basit's, for there were only three fisher-cats to be seen. But they were well-built specimens, walking proudly in line with tails erect, each carrying in its mouth a fine, fat fish. Already we had evidence that we were not quite alone on the island.

In the Muhafaza itself, exploration was limited by the fact that our only artificial light was a pressurised paraffin lamp which, once pumped up and lit, hissed menacingly and gave forth a sickly greenish light that could do no more than hold the shadows at arm's length. Nevertheless it sufficed, and we were able to discover a small wooden chest containing photographs and documents. The most interesting picture was inscribed 'Osman Digna, redoubtable leader of the Sudanese Arabs, finally captured on 13th January 1900 at Warriba.'

The lamp hissed on and on, its unceasing sound punctuated from time to time by a thud from outside – doubtless falling masonry. We loved that evening for its utter peace and solitude. Margaret set about copying the photograph – the sketch is before me now. It shows a very carefully composed group, in which the individuals are placed according to importance, as in ancient Nilotic art. The most conspicuous figure is a stout gentleman in full military attire complete with bandolier: Margaret's pencilled note explains that he is the Turk who captured Osman. Osman Digna himself stands somewhat further back, his right hand held behind him in an attempt to conceal the fact that he is chained to a military nonentity in the background. His turbanned face is kindly and fringed with a Father Christmas-like beard, and it comes as a surprise to read in Margaret's notes that he was 'distinguished in battle and of the tribe that once broke a British "square"'. He wears a smock somewhat reminiscent of west country cider revels, with baggy trousers of the plus-fours variety that complete the impression of the benevolent old country gentleman.

While Margaret drew I perused a stack of notes she had prepared from a series of volumes entitled *Sudan Notes and Records*. It was fascinating to see how the material in the chest dovetailed with her earlier gleanings. The documents accompanying the photographs were mostly burial records of the Suakin Cemetery between 1884 and 1932: names, nationalities, occupations and causes of death. Bit by bit in a strange way, it seemed as if the evidence from these two sources breathed the vigour of life into the deserted ruins that surrounded us. We decided that our architectural students, if not aware of their Suakin inheritance, ought to have the opportunity to become better informed. So, forthwith, I wrote an exercise for them, calling it 'Suakin Besieged'.

The key figure of this exercise was Richard Wake who is buried in grave 207. He was an artist on the staff of *The Graphic*, aged 24, who was shot near the Water Forts during the great siege. Having introduced him, as Margaret drew busily away on the far side of the seething lamp, in imagination I tried to transport myself back to the Suakin of seventy-five years before, and I wrote something like this:

> 'What fantastic sights he must have seen; what strange pictures he must have drawn! Suakin, "the very daughter of the sea", with its lime-coloured coralline walls; the street that was taken up almost entirely with hairdressers' shops for the Beja tribesmen; the fine Turkish doorways; the richly fretted windows painted in red and green; the throngs of traders and camels; the mosques, minarets, palaces. Richard Wake might well have witnessed the arrival of General Sartorious accompanied by his wife and step-daughter. What a stir these

*Imaginary scene in Suakin including Mrs and Miss Sartorious in the foreground*

*Mrs. and Miss Sartorious, drawn from contemporary photograph*

European females must have caused; how strange their nineteenth-century English finery must have looked in these surroundings! And in his time, too, HMS *Ranger* and HMS *Woodlark*, and the gunboart *Coquette*, docked in the harbour. Perhaps he made drawings of the demonstrations of shellfire given at night by the warships, the effect of which seems to have been not to reassure but to give fresh cause for alarm to the besieged inhabitants.'

Then came the meat of the exercise:

'Imagine a scene in the besieged town, including, if possible, Mrs. and Miss Sartorious – or – imagine a night view, with shellfire and the moon illuminating the town. Then DRAW one of these scenes.'

I knew the students would not lack material. In addition to our own drawings and photographs, they would be able to find prints showing handsome ships of the period, and plenty of illustrations of nineteenth century European ladies' clothes – a branch of architectural study which I rightly guessed they would find fascinating.

Pleasantly tired, we went next door to slip into our lightweight sleeping bags and lie in delicious comfort on our *angareebs*– divan-style beds with string mattresses that are used almost universally in the Sudan.

Sleep came quickly, and how long it was before the ghost arrived we couldn't say. The moon had gone, and in the pitch darkness we only managed to knock the lamp over without discovering the whereabouts of the matches or torch. Meanwhile the ghost was pacing up and down outside the bedroom door. I blundered about in the darkness trying to find the door in order to see – or not to see – the intruder. My efforts failed – perhaps they were only half hearted. Instead I rediscovered my sleeping bag and shook mysef back into it. Nothing happened; we must have dropped off. And the whole idea of ghosts evaporated in the clear light of the gorgeous morning that greeted us on waking.

A few days later we walked along the quayside of the dhow anchorage, past the ruins of the ginning factory, until we saw facing us across the lagoon the remains of the Caravanserai. This building was, in effect, a combined hotel, store and workshop for the reception and housing of camel caravans such as those still to be seen making their way to the Red Sea from the far west of the Sudan. It was still in fairly good shape, for although many doors and windows had disappeared or decayed into shapeless voids, all of its four storeys were still standing.

It was only after we had spent some time gazing intently at this crumbling mass mirrored in the lagoon, that we realised we were not alone. A boat full of fishing nets was moored at the water's edge, and close by sat a dejected looking man who we concluded must be its owner.

We greeted him in Arabic: 'Es salaam aleikum' – Peace be with you, to which he responded and then continued in English. He invited us to sit with him; and we soon learned that he was a fisherman from Port Sudan. Gratefully he shared our cheese and mango, and then he embarked on a curious tale.

He began by relating how, in Port Sudan, he had fallen for a damsel who did not respond to his advances. So desperately in love was he that he went to a magician or astrologer in the market, from whom he demanded a really powerful love potion. The magician told him to catch a large bat – of the fruit-eating variety common in cultivated areas of the Sudan – bake it in the sun and pulverise it. The resulting powder was to be given over to the magician who, for a fee, would mix it with certain magical substances of his own. The fisherman was assured that the resulting concoction, if properly used, would certainly have the desired result.

'Did you do it?' 'Oh, yes, indeed I did. I paid him plenty.'

From the man's tone and his downcast air, we gathered that things had not gone well. And so he went on to explain.

The magician had indeed produced the promised ingredients which he had mixed with the bat powder. We got the impression that the 'goo' thus produced was pretty tacky and nasty stuff, with a powerful stink. Handing over the tin, the magician warned the fisherman that not only would its contents seduce the lady, but it was such potent stuff that *anybody* who came in contact with it would fall madly in love with him.

The fisherman was in the habit of calling on his beloved at a certain time in the evening, announcing his arrival by a certain 'rat-a-ty-tat-tat' which she always recognised. And although she obstinately withheld her love, she never failed to open the door to him.

Feverish with expectation, the fisherman approached the girl's house, stopping only to daub the black mess liberally over his palms and wrists. He performed his customary tattoo, but in one respect he departed crucially from precedent. Always before, he had called late in the day; but now, unable to wait, he was knocking on the door in mid-morning. Things went terribly wrong. Instead of the young lady, it was an enormous male servant who flung open the door. 'Es salaam aleikum,' the servant cried. At that he grabbed both the fisherman's hands, squeezing so hard that the 'goo' squelched out all over his own hands and forearms.

Terrified at the thought of the obvious result of his action, the fisherman turned and fled, not stopping until he reached his boat. He dared not return; so instead he made his way south to Suakin.

'He was really *hideous*.' The fisherman looked dismally across the blue waters of the lagoon, and shuddered.

Before we parted we arranged to meet again the next day. Perhaps we would eat together at the Muhafaza. But when we returned, there was no trace of him or his boat. The undisturbed sand supplied no clue. We scanned the lagoon, peering out beyond Condensor Island to the outer harbour until our eyes watered in the sunny glare. Nothing!

When we returned to Khartoum, Basit was waiting. We lost no time in telling him that we had seen the cats, and that although we had not seen a ghost we had certainly heard one. And for good measure, we had a story about sorcery. . . .

Basit listened imperturbably. The ghost he passed over, but he fastened on the story of the fisherman.

'All that happened to that fisherman,' he patiently explained, 'was that he had the misfortune to consult a wicked wali. Mostly such persons are said to be Nigerian.' (We had already gathered that Nigerians were sometimes credited with occult powers – even to the extent of being able to influence the results of football matches). 'But it is a heathen practice and considered anti-Islam. For the Sudanese it is a bit of a disgrace to go to such people.'

Having delivered his verdict in suitably judicial terms, he added a more informal rider.

'The wicked *walis* by threats attempt to convince you of their powers. A very effective psychological move. But to be honest I do not believe in them.'

I guessed that as he hadn't believed in the ghostly footsteps, he didn't believe in the ghost. He had explanations for most things. Then a sudden thought struck him.

'Perhaps,' he said, 'you may be interested to hear of a story concerning my aunty.'

'Wonderful, Basit – but another time. Right now I have a little surprise for you and the others – to help you share with us something of the history and beauty of Suakin. It's an exercise, and it's called "Suakin Besieged"'. And then and there I handed out a copy to each of the students.

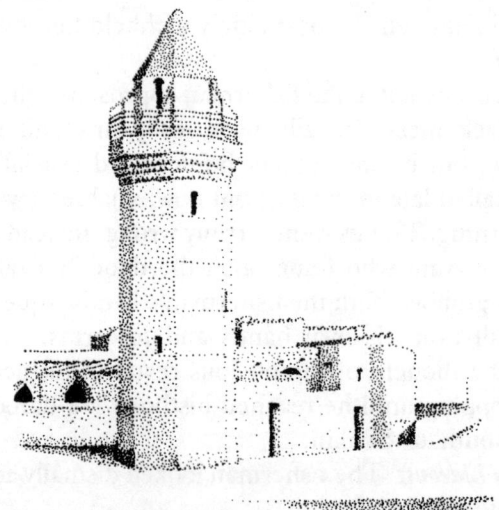

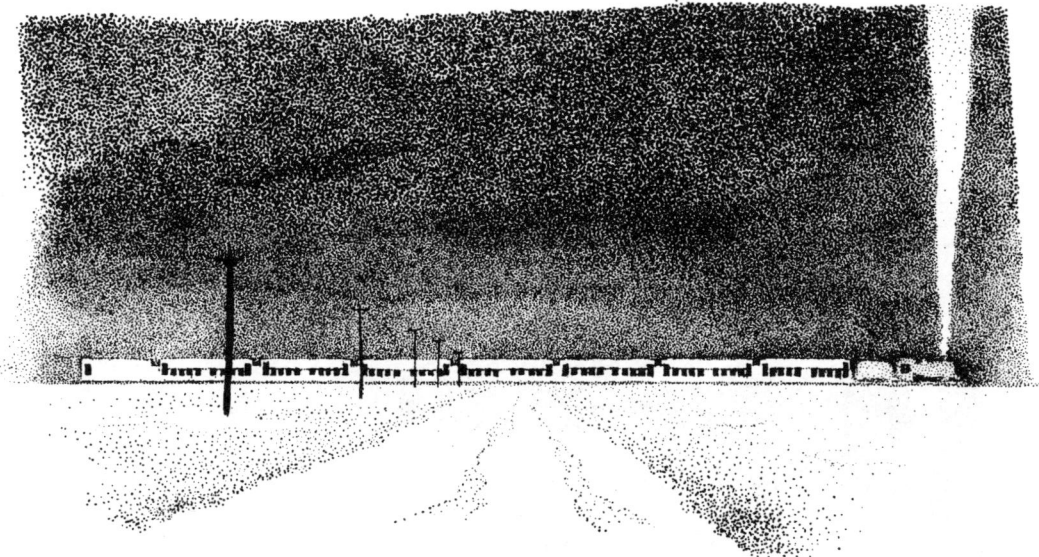

# 15 Nubie

It was hardly likely that anyone would drop into my office in the morning hours between seven and nine. What was quite unthinkable was that any total stranger should burst in upon that pre-breakfast period of calm and concentration.

Yet that is exactly what happened on that particular day. I was wrestling with a pile of application forms for entry to the Department, inhaling the methylated spirit with which the duplicating process had impregnated them and marvelling at the resourcefulness with which some candidates had risen to the challenge of filling in the white spaces left for the answers. For instance, there was the question: 'Connections, (family or otherwise), with the architectural profession or building industry?'. Against this one Sayed Abdalla el Radi had pencilled in a firm hand, 'I have no connection, except with my eyes!'

Perhaps it was my absorption in el Radi's answers, perhaps it was the alcoholic cloud of duplicating fluid in which I was working, and undoubtedly the visitor's thick-soled track shoes had something to do with it – but whatever the reason, I was totally unaware of my visitor until he was there in front of me. He did not arrive, he materialized. As my eyes left the paper I became aware of a pair of white masculine legs supported on massive platforms of spongy sole; of voluminous shorts which belied their name, for they came down to mid-knee level; of a shirt which challenged my preconceptions of a lifetime by being draped over the shorts and not tucked in at the waist; and of a cap with a positively enormous peak which now swivelled like a blue searchlight in my direction.

*The Sudan Museum with (left) a corner of the Department of Architecture*

'I take it you're the boss of this outfit? I already took the liberty of inspecting some of your exhibits.'

The stranger's voice was kindly, somewhat modifying the impression of agressiveness created by his clothes. But whatever could he mean? The Department of Architecture had no exhibition, no models, not even any drawings on display. The absurd thought flashed through my mind that we had nothing better to offer in the way of an object of interest or admiration than our messenger Daoud, who sat by the front door knitting himself ear muffs against the dreaded onset of winter.

But the stranger continued:

'Mind you, I'd been expecting more mummies, fewer potsherds.'

Now it clear what had happened – he was off course. He thought he was in the old Sudan Museum which occupied the handsome structure standing cheek by jowl with our own modest building. His assumption that he was talking to a boss showed discrimination. A less observant soul might have asked where he could find the director. My heart began to warm to this misplaced human being.

'Have a lemoon, or a coffee,' I suggested; and, eyeing the photographic equipment with which he was festooned, I added, 'take the weight off your feet. Let's sit . . . You must be interested in antiquities.'

'Yeah. I guess you'd think that. The time I spent in your museum.'

His descent of a steep hill of false assumptions was gathering momentum. I watched for a chance to halt him. A momentary pause gave me the chance to introduce myself and my department. Having done so I succumbed to the missionary spirit of my calling by volunteering advice on what Khartoum and the Sudan had to offer by way of architectural delights; and having talked of temples, pyramids, sculptures and tombs, something made me add, 'Nubia is beautiful, don't miss Nubia.'

'Nubia. Funny you should mention Nubia. That's the place I really want to see. In fact, if it wasn't for Nubia, I wouldn't be here at all.'

At that time relatively little had been done to excavate and publicise the archaeological riches of Nubia, to celebrate its history or encapsulate its strange beauty in handsome picture books. That anyone not already a fully-fledged specialist of some sort should want to visit this out-of-the-way corner of the African sub-continent seemed, to say the least, somewhat odd. He must have guessed the way my mind was working, for almost immediately he continued.

'I guess you're curious: why Nubia? Well, it's kinda personal. Not private, though – anyone can know. And since you're interested in Nubia, I'll tell you . . . you see, my son's called Nubie.'

I was not sure that I did see.

'Nubie, that's an unusual name even in . . .'

I stopped. So far the stranger hadn't unburdened himself concerning his country of origin.

'Yeah!' I'm thinking maybe that son of mine is the only person in the whole world with that particular name. We were both after something distinctive by way of a name, the missus and me. But the time went on and we hadn't decided on anything special. So you won't be surprised, we turned to the Lord for Enlightenment.'

Perhaps my face showed more surprise than he had bargained for. His own assumed a grave expression.

'I don't know whether you believe in God, Mr. Potter, like we do where I come from. In the natural course the old folk sought guidance from the Good Book. They'd open it as the Spirit directed. And then the Hand of God, acting of course through them, his creatures, would guide them to find Enlightenment.'

I could have sworn there was for a split second a humorous twinkle in his eyes. But he sounded solemn enough as he went on.

*Grapefruit*

'But, Mr. Potter, God helps best those that help themselves. So we decided to try a modified version of the old method. We didn't use the Good Book. But we chose a big one. And a modern one. That way we decided the Direction should be good and fresh.'

He paused.

'You're wondering what that big book might have been?'

I was!

At that he walked over to one of the windows. The outer shutters were pinned back, and the pair of inner casements was folded to the white painted plaster, revealing the Department's grove of grapefruit trees, their dark leaves untroubled by the least breath of wind, their innumerable clusters of green fruit touched shyly by the new day's sun. Mechanically, it seemed, but methodically the stranger selected a lens from his profusion of photographic paraphernalia, fitted it into his camera, read an exposure, made adjustments, focussed and pressed. His mission accomplished, he prowled toward the armchair I had earlier indicated and, having shifted various items of equipment around his body so as to ensure a soft landing, subsided into its embrace.

'I guess I'm about ready for that lemon drink you mentioned.'

I clapped. Daoud entered smartly – he must have stowed away his knitting in a flash. He was swinging his old tin tray and smiling his customary infectious smile: it was the face of one who is utterly unconcrned about 'keeping up with the Mohammeds.'

The order was given in Arabic: 'Itnain lemoon, minfadlak, aiwa?'

And the reply came, 'Aiwa, kuwayyis jiddan' – OK, jolly good! To Daoud life always appeared as 'kuwayyis jiddan' – the tops.

'You were saying . . . about that Big Book . . . and God,' I prompted.

'Yeah.'

For a time he gave no further answer. Instead he took the film out of his camera: his last 'snap' must have completed the spool. Tiny unchivalrous doubts assailed me. Was he reluctant to complete his tale? Did he fear that it would turn out to be a damp squib? But at last the spool was stowed away, and quietly he went on.

'Mmm. The Big Book. Just an Atlas – a mighty big one. Having chosen the book the rest was simple. Grace takes my right hand in her left. And our hands together move around the printed page. But a Power directs us – you understand?'

He pointed straight above him, to where the big electric fan hung swaying on its rod, growling at every turn a threat of decapitation for those below.

'Africa north of the Equator, the map was called. After a bit of circling over the page, our hands came to a halt right where the name NUBIA was printed. So then and there we decided to call the kid Nubie, after the country. So now you see why I'm here – to have a dekko at the place.'

Wafts of mild air from the fan enveloped us both: the shared pleasure drew us together. Outside, Daoud could be heard approaching along the gravel path, the tinkling of ice against the sides of the pint-sized glasses already audible.

He entered, and I thanked him: 'Shukran gazeelan. Bismillahi' – in the name of God.

The drink was cool, rich with the flavour of many fresh limes and much cane sugar. Relaxed and refreshed, I let my thoughts float to Nubia, its black-robed countrywomen, their puzzling ancient homes, the morning light on Nile water foaming over rocks.

Then I heard myself saying: 'God moves in a mysterious way.' It was the best I could manage. 'And', I added, 'He made a great job of helping you to choose.'

'You think so?' He seemed relieved at the way I had reacted to his confidences. 'I think tomorrow I'll be leaving for the North by train. I understand they're pretty good.'

'Well' – I spoke from experience – 'there are four classes. 'First' is pretty luxurious, the others less so, as you'd expect. What 'Fourth' lacks in plumbing it makes up for in local colour, and,' – I said, bearing in mind the camera kit – 'that's something you might like.'

'But', I added emphatically, '*no toilets*. The train stops pretty often instead. It's flat and there are no trees. But it gives you a chance.'

'You think I'd manage OK?'

I eyed the voluminous shorts.

'You'd have your problems . . .' How sensible, I reflected, was the Sudanese garb. There flitted through my mind images of squatting figures, each ensconced in a tent-like *gellabiya* or *tobe*, and each with a far-away look in the eyes.

'Before travelling north by fourth class, better buy yourself a *gellabiya*. That's my advice.'

At breakfast Margaret listened intently to my account of what had happened in the past hour.

'He seems a nice chap, your stranger. You know, of course, that most of the time he was pulling your leg.'

Perhaps . . . we'll never know. Still, if the story is a true one, Nubie was in good company. His parents' method of choosing a name was not so very different from the way in which Mohammed decided on the site for a house. Plagued with indecision, he determined to leave the choice to Allah. His riding camel was allowed to roam free; it came to a halt in the middle of an oasis where dates were laid out to dry. Mohammed dismounted. Allah had shown that this was to be the site of his house.

## 16 The Resident Engineer & The Huq

It was with a sense of deep contentment that, one Sunday morning, I sat ensconced in an armchair in the office of the university's Resident Engineer, Sayed Hassan el Bahar. I knew that he must already have pressed the secret electric button to summon his white-robed *suffragi*, who would reappear a little later with his tin tray laden with glasses of lemoon, small tumblers of tea or *'tanakas'* of coffee. Awaiting this refreshment, I drank in the flute-like descending scales of countless birds which floated on the still air from near and far to mingle with the drone of the fan hanging from the brick vault above me; and I watched half-mesmerised as the sun, stealthy and pale as yet, dappled the floor with its proof of the promise made to me in London: 'the finest winter climate in the world'.

It was one of those moments when, as the hymn says,'every prospect pleases'; but my state of euphoria flowed also from deeper sources. For I now found myself, within a few weeks of our arrival in the Sudan, practising architecture as well as teaching it. I had been commissioned to convert a students' union – and heaven knows what it had been before that – into a zoological museum. Strangely enough, little structural change was required; and it was a relief not to have to hack away at a building of such quality as this one. Not only its forms but its materials – pinkish ashlar masonry walls and a reddish clay tile roof – marked it off from the majority of buildings of the Three Towns of Khartoum, Omdurman and Khartoum North; yet its individuality did not brashly proclaim itself but was discreetly veiled by shrubs and flowering trees, so that it consorted easily with the attractive university administration buildings that were its neighbours.

It was a fascinating job; yet even more welcome than the work itself was the contact that it brought with Hassan. He was everyone's friend – well, almost everyone's. There were a few among the expatriate staff I fancied, who saw Hassan merely as a functionary, who did not know how he loved people and how readily he succumbed to laughter, his deep brown features suddenly corrugating, his large, close cropped, grizzled head jerked back and his tusk-like teeth protruding. To these few, he was simply the one who should be blamed when their switches clicked unavailingly, when their waste-pipes over-flowed or when Hassan's minions carried out 'repairs' which made matters worse rather than better.

Not even the picture which almost covered the wall behind Hassan's desk could cast a chill over his hospitality. Fully a metre wide and rather less in height, it was clearly the work of a 'Sunday painter'. But I was always riveted by the incisiveness of its chalk and brush strokes, and by the unmistakable urge to communicate a message that had possessed the artist – a title I could not deny him despite all his shortcomings of technique. From first to last, it was a picture that set out to tell a story – one so horrible that it demanded attention. On one side white soldiers, no doubt British, in old-fashioned uniforms were viciously hammering the heads of black-skinned men; in another part of the picture the blacks had just put to flight a wounded and bedraggled force of whites; and the space around and between these two centres of action was filled with the paraphernalia of battle. So there we sat, bathed in birdsong, broken sunshine and fraternal feeling, I with my orange *mercub* (old men's slippers, my students called them) extended almost to sprawling point, Hassan genially shunting papers as a preliminary to our talk, while all the time this fantastic backdrop of ancient animosities glowed with defunct passion behind him.

Most of Hassan's papers needed no more than a glance before he shot them unerringly into one or another of a series of 'pending' trays, most of which were already uncomfortably full. There, I suspected, many would rest collecting sand for months while Hassan and his acolytes – carpenters, bricklayers, electricians – went on grappling with the near-impossible: going the rounds of a vast assortment of university buildings, patching them up and (what he really enjoyed) trying to keep the occupants happy. Paper work was not Hassan's strong point, but he had an unrivalled knowledge of building contractors in the Three Towns and a vast fund of practical experience.

Not surprisingly, these contacts and this expertise had now brought him face to face with a dilemma which he gleefully unfolded to me. He had been invited to enter into partnership with a contractor to provide some kind of irrigation channels for farmers in the Gezira cotton growing area. The essence of the scheme was the 'know-how' that Hassan could contribute – at a profit. 'Eighty piastres we can charge, and that they could easily do for themselves for twenty piastres,' he explained. The idea of so much for so little was ludicrous; absurdity begat hilarity, which in turn begat more hilarity, and before long I was having to mop up lemoon which had sullied the gleaming white perfection of my outfit.

Yet for all the laughter, a small shadow had come across our clear sky; for I knew that if Hassan were to go, life in the university would lose some of its richness and we would be the poorer for the ending of an infant friendship. But I should have known: in talking to me, Hassan was getting this temptation out of his system. For him to leave us would really be unthinkable; and it did not happen.

From this never-to-be-realised daydream, our conversation veered at last to the avowed subject of my visit; the conversion of the old students' union building. Soon we got into Hassan's huge American car, whose age was as uncertain as its colour – for wind-blown sand had scoured off most of its paint – and with engine coughing and growling rebelliously as Hassan drove with minimum use of clutch and gears, we skirted the western bank of the Blue Nile. By now the sun was riding high, casting a

*The Huq*

neatly circular shadow of intense black round the bole of every riverside tree, where such grew isolated from their companions. And across the blue-green waters it blazed its fiery trails.

Inside the union building it was comparatively dark and cool, for the windows had been shuttered against heat and intruders. Sand covered everything: broken chairs, tables and *angareeb* which had been gathered into great piles on the floor, and its sweet, not unpleasant smell filled the place. It was amongst all this desolation that I found the *Huq*.

I spotted the first bit of it sticking out from under an *angareeb*. After the dust had been rubbed away a spindle-like wooden stand could be seen. It was beautifully turned, with a profile that spoke of a hand not only highly skilled but unerringly commanded by a mind attuned to beauty. As in the mouldings of Greek temples, each element of the whole was complete in itself. Like the scotias, cymas and cavettos of the classical orders, each of its shapes possessed a point of departure and of conclusion; yet in the whole there was not a single note of discord. Intuitively the artist-craftsman had achieved a unity that would have satisfied the most fastidious sixteenth-century Florentine critic.

As we poked about, more and more pieces came to light until we found that in addition to the large spindle we had three smaller turned pieces and four wooden cups with lids that fitted. Every piece had been turned on a lathe, and the work – I was at a loss to think of a word for it – had originally been brightly painted with stripes of brick-red, cadmium yellow and black. It was not difficult to see how the bits fitted together, and when we had assembled them all we found that we had a stand with three arms projecting horizontally in different directions about half way up the spindle, with an empty hole where there had evidently been a fourth arm. We slotted three of the cups into place at the end of the arms, where they were obviously meant to go, keeping the fourth cup for the moment in reserve.

'That', announced Hassan, 'is a *Huq*.'

'Whatever is that, Hassan?'

'Well, it was used by Arab ladies in olden times. You used to be able to buy such things in Omdurman. But', he added sadly, 'no longer now . . .' Then he went on.

'And the Arab ladies kept their senses in them.'

'Senses, Hassan, whatever were senses?'

'Senses, you know senses. Your European ladies, they keep their senses in bottles . . . makes them smell good.' Seeing that light was only just beginning to dawn he embarked on further explanation.

'Our senses are gums, woods and seeds. And these they would separate and store inside the cups you see upon the *Huq*. Sometimes if they wanted to smell good, they would choose senses from the Hoag and burn them slowly. And now they would take off their closes and crouch low over the smouldering senses and make some sort of blanket cover to make it better . . .'

'That was good!'

He closed his eyes and breathed in deeply in imagination sniffing long dead perfumes, an ageing man re-capturing the freshness of puberty.

'Yes,' he resumed after a silence, '. . . they would go to bed then and be ready for you. And it was good, very good.'

His eyes twinkled. We were back in the present.

'If Margaret would like to know such things, you tell her: Go to Mekki'.

'What! Mekki Shibeika, our Pro-Vice Chancellor?' It would never have struck me that this scholarly Arab historian, possessor of doctorates, author of many books and countless articles, would also be an authority on these matters.

Then Hassan had second thoughts:

'No! Better Margaret not go to Mekki. Better she go to Mekki's wife.'

'Marvellous!' I said, and I meant it.

At that, back I trudged on foot to Sharia el Gamhuria, bursting to tell Margaret about the new-found treasure that I carried tenderly under my arm.

Next morning, after breakfast, the sound of clapping hands reached us through the grove of grapefruit and orange trees which separated our house from the road. This was the usual way of announcing one's presence in a country as yet unequipped with doorbells. Going to the front of the house, we found Hassan, attended by two of his acolytes and holding a small parcel in his hands.

'The *Huq* was incomplete,' he said. 'One arm was missing, and I have had it turned. See, here it is.' And as he took off the wrapping paper, he added 'The paint may not be quite the same. But Margaret, she is good with such things – she can quickly touch it.'

Then we noticed that each of the acolytes was carrying two parcels. Seeing that we had noticed them, Hassan gently took the four packages from their hands and deposited them in Margaret's.

'Senses,' he explained. 'Now you can put them in your Huq'.

And there they still are. Each wooden cup still holds the contents of its own special package; each still possesses the individual slip of paper, pencilled at the time, to describe its own 'sense' –

Luban (lumps of gum); Bakhour (a mix of gums and woods); el Timan (another mix); Talihe (tree bark).

*A spray of oleander*

*Dr Wenzel's puppets*

# 17 Dr Wenzel takes the biscuit

It took a little time to understand why our university colleagues from Yugoslavia spoke with such admiration, even awe, of Marian Wenzel. This tall and comely young woman with a mane of raven black hair parted in the middle and a creamish complexion starred with eyes of limpid brown that beamed intelligence and impishness at you, was certainly someone you would never overlook. But how could this youngster in her mid-twenties have acquired a scholarly reputation, in the field of art history, weighty enough to impress our fellow academics?

Bit by bit we learned the answer to this riddle: stories of how she had travelled on donkey-back to ancient cemeteries to search, measure, think and type by day, and to sleep under the stars in her extra-long sleeping bag by night; and how, in due course, her observations and deductions about these near-prehistoric tombstones had been embodied in a report written in impeccable Serbo-Croat.

Needless to say, supper Chez Marian was always memorable. But there was one particular evening, the last we ever spent with her in Khartoum, that impressed itself indelibly on our minds; for it was then that she gave us the first inkling of a path down (or up) which her questing intellect was about to lead her: a long, long path, beginning in Nubia and ending in a most surprisingly different place.

The evening began placidly enough. Having mounted the rough-cast steps of Marian's newly-built house on the outermost fringes of the city, we paid our customary homage to her home-made puppets strung lop-headed and somewhat spookily from huge nails bashed by the doctor's own fair hand into the lime-washed walls. The meal over, we sat on the balcony on chairs of mahogany and chintz, sniffing the aroma of incipient coffee and enjoying to the full the sensation of being armchair travellers; for from the balcony the view was of the hot black emptiness of the Sahara – a thousand miles of nothingness stretching halfway across the belly of Africa and interrupted only by the Sudanese town of El Fasher a little to our left. Imagination transported us over endless seas of sand to the first havens of human habitation in the Lake Chad basin; and for companionship on our journey we lazily leafed through a familiar publication, *Investigation of Buildings in Wadi Halfa and Adjoining Villages*, written by our students as the record of their first-ever trek in the district four years before. We smiled as we read the European-sounding observation: 'Planning complications were never introduced to make a building look different from what it was meant to be'; and we congratulated ourselves afresh that our students had not overlooked the wall-paintings with which the Nubians decorated their homes.

Marian's voice came floating through our thoughts, uncannily in tune with what we had just been reading. It was – and is – a musical voice, its north American substratum thinly overlaid and enriched by tonal and verbal encrustations from many out-of-the-way places, yet without any trace of artifice or artificiality. 'The first time I heard about Nubian house decorations was from George Shiner, the head of the New Mexico expedition stationed in Wadi Halfa which was working on prehistoric monuments. I asked him how the decorations originated, and he said that all of them felt that they must have a very long history. But, as he pointed out, his team was there to work on really ancient things, and it had no finance for other pursuits'.

'And', Margaret chimed in, 'every blessed soul said just the same to us. Everyone seems certain that these decorative styles can be traced right back – to Tutankhamun and before.'

Did I detect a slight note of weariness, even bitterness in her voice? She had spent the previous fortnight designing and making a huge cotton wallhanging with appliquéd Nubian-style decorations; and her ancient sewing machine had been playing her up.

'What do *you* think, Marian?' Margaret went on. 'Is the whole business a recent invention?'

Marian reflected. 'My bet is, it is and it isn't. When Burckhardt came exploring in the Sudan at Nubia in 1813 there were certainly no paintings visible then. Nor were there when the other early travellers were about. I assure you I've gone carefully through everything they've published – nothing! Some of the ideas used by modern house-painters may be based on ancient myths . . . but however they originated, they *are* fantastic, aren't they?'

As if by way of consolation for what she was about to say, she pressed us to partake of more of the Yugoslavian fire-water that she thoughtfully imported for her guests; and as I dreamily noted that we had managed to reduce the level to the half-way mark, she explained to us that although we had seen something of these Nubian decorations on our way to Semna and Abu Simbel, there was much that we had missed through not being able to deviate from our track to right or left. As she talked, visions of these unseen riches formed themselves against the starlit sky, to be dispelled abruptly by an even more arresting vision which suddenly manifested itself – Marian's long-haired snow-white cat, Poosey Kadisa, standing alert on the parapet before us, bushing her huge squirrel's tail and turning to reveal the diamanté necklace without which she never appeared in public.

Soon after that evening we left Khartoum for India, never to return for more than a brief stay. From time to time our ex-students, some of whom seemed to spend more time in Europe than in Africa, brought us snippets of news of Marian: that the University had provided funds for fresh expeditions and fresh researches; and that she had also been studying in England. But we were hungry for more; and it was with the keenest anticipation that we waited, at long last, for her to join us for a holiday in Wales.

We had no balcony to offer her with a view over the Sahara; a slate roof overhead replaced the star-studded Khartoum sky; and a log fire blazed defiance at the bleakness beyond the windows, fighting duels with draughts, keeping the invading chill at bay with its crackling threats and enfolding us precariously in a tiny buffer-state of warmth that never for a moment recalled the all-pervading despotism of the Sudanese sun. But Marian herself was just the same as ever, bubbling with high spirits and overflowing with anecdotes. It was only her unfamiliar dress that we had to get used to: no longer the black *gerger* worn by Nubian ladies, but a dark-hued robe of unusual length, decorated with a frontal pattern of gold beads and gems that would surely have been approved by Sudanese ladies.

As Marian had half suspected before her research began in earnest, it proved that no really old house decorations existed in Nubia. The earliest examples, all fragmentary, could be assigned only to the turn of the century; and there was not a shred of evidence that the decorative traditions of Nubia survived from ancient times. Some of the older paintings had been done by women, who had found time on their hands while their husbands and brothers were working as cooks in Cairo and Khartoum – a calling for which Nubians seem to have a special aptitude, and in which not a few achieved distinction. All this Marian found out by talking to grandmothers about their own and their forebears' experiences. Grandfathers, it seemed, were thinner on the ground and far less communicative: perhaps they were not anxious to recall in precise detail how they had fared in the fleshpots of the big cities, during their time of lucrative exile before they returned to their domestic circles.

Gradually Marian was forced to a surprising conclusion: that the real flowering of Nubian mural art had come only during the Nineteen-Twenties. And what had caused the desert to flower was, basically, the gentle showers of cash from relations in Egypt and Khartoum. At first, this money financed 'do-it-yourself' activities; but before long the ladies began to commission wall-decorators and house builders. To begin with, the villagers found inspiration for their decorative styles in the everyday objects that surrounded them. But the later work, much of it done by professionals, seemed at first an inscrutable mystery: where on earth had this sophisticated and fascinating style originated, and how had it developed?

*Entrance incorporating saucers embedded in mud construction – popular form of decoration*

*The* diwani

It was to the unravelling of this conundrum that Marian now devoted herself. Most of the professional decorators were no longer in business, but fortunately a few remained. One of them in particular proved a mine of information. Hassan Araby was not merely a fine artist; he was tall, handsome in a Mediterranean way, and highly intelligent; and some of the ladies he had worked for were full of praise for him and his work. One of these told Marian how he had very beautifully decorated her *diwani* in tones of orange, adorning it with baskets of flowers and the long-legged birds he loved to paint, and tying the entire composition together by extremely elaborate geometric borders. 'The lady became quite giggly', said Marian, 'when she told me about his working habits. She was not allowed to enter while he was actually at work, but he liked to have refreshments brought to him from time to time; and as he painted he would sing, most seductively, "I'm going to make a palace for you – you are so beautiful".'

From anecdote Marian passed rapidly to analysis. 'That *diwani*', she said, 'was one of the best examples of Hassan's Geometric phase, before the Art Deco phase began'. She went on to explain that the geometric phase, with its squares (some of them containing superimposed patterns), its semi-circles, arches, flags, triangles, and its long-legged birds, owed nothing to sources outside Nubia. But the succeeding phase, the one Marian had dubbed 'Art Deco', was quite different. Hassan's decorative motifs became light-ray shapes, cones of light, beams, zig-zags, parallel bars, stepped pyramids and erratic angular shapes.

When Marian grilled Hassan concerning the sources of these mysterious symbols he was strangely reticent and vague, giving her the impression that she might do worse than take a hard look at Egyptian towels of fifty or sixty years ago, at Cairo newspapers of the 'thirties and 'forties, and also at old tins. Many a research worker might have been daunted by such answers – but not Marian. Was there not a tradition that of the explorers of Darkest Africa, it was the ladies who had been the most intrepid of all?

The idea that Egyptian towels could have survived several decades of use, and then be in a fit state to inspire Hassan's artistic output, seemed so wildly improbable that Marian had little hesitation in rejecting it.

'But', said Marian, 'newspapers and magazines were a different matter – it was perfectly possible to see what they had to offer because there are quite a lot of them in the oriental and Islamic section of the British Library in London. They proved disappointing, however– just a few necktie advertisements, concentric circles and sunrays, and even these faded out as the war began to hot up. So I turned to tins. There were only three sorts: petrol, treacle and biscuit. Petrol tins weren't decorated, so they were out. Treacle, too – they never changed, just an old lion very much asleep. So I was left with other kinds of food tins, and of these biscuits seemed much the best bet: they were just the sort of things that cooks in Cairo or Khartoum might send home as presents. So I wrote round to a variety of biscuit manufacturers, getting no reply except from Huntley and Palmers. The head of their publicity, Michael Paxton, told me that his firm had been the leading exporter of biscuits to the Sudan – and a good many other parts too, and he invited me to pay them a visit at their factory at Reading.'

It was time to feed the fire with more dry logs, which it received with grateful spluttering; and soon a delicious resinous odour filled every corner of the room. We tilted our glasses of clear, fermented blackberry juice, and Marian embarked on the conclusion of her Nubian narrative.

'They let me examine their annual catalogue, a lavish affair, which they've issued every year since 1900 – *Huntley and Palmers Christmas biscuits and cakes*. Each one showed every biscuit tin you could buy at Christmas, year by year. Just think of that!'

We duly thought, as a little more blackberry trickled down.

'And of course it was quite simple', Marian went on, a note of elation now discernible. 'It was like a miniature history of a branch of commercial art. Roughly speaking, ordinary biscuits went into fairly ordinary tins; but at Christmas there were, of course, lots of special lines – gift packages with exotic contents. When Art Deco came in, it wasn't long before the firm's more frivolous tins – usually for their more way-out products such as cocktail biscuits – followed suit: the whole paraphernalia, pyramids, jagged sunrays, and so forth. They carried on with Art Deco up to 1940, when it was dropped as being too giddy for wartime.'

'Now, all Hassan's Art Deco houses were built a few years before or after the terrible Nile floods of 1948. You might say, then, that the dates don't fit. But of course there's a time lag: first comes export, then purchase, then consumption, then cherishing, then maybe discarding – and there the tins are at last, ready to inspire an artist who has worked out one vein and is looking for another.'

She paused again, while I thought of the strange contrast between the polished red brickwork of Reading and the 'simple, smooth plastic mud' villages described by our students in the Wadi Halfa report. But in Marian's company, reveries were never protracted. I suddenly realised that she was telling us of the marvels of Huntley and Palmers biscuit museum: how you could actually see the beautiful tins, and gaze on the biscuits that had won gold medals at international exhibitions.

'They were kept under glass, and they looked as if you could actually eat them.' We had no doubt that Marian, ever avid for knowledge, would have succumbed to temptation if she had been offered a wee nibble. 'They even had the actual biscuit which saved a soldier's life at the Battle of Omdurman in 1898 . . . mind you it did look pretty hard tack.' Which we were not surprised to hear, if indeed it had deflected a Mahdist bullet.

Her story had reached its conclusion – but there was a coda. Swiftly and in muted but ever richer voice, Marian told us how, not surprisingly, Huntley and Palmers were surprised and gratified to find that, thanks to her, they now occupied a niche in the history of art. Her revelation of how commerce had been the inadvertent handmaiden of culture led to a fresh invitation to Reading, this time to see their latest creations, which included an amazing array of wedding cake and an entire battle scene made of sugar. After that there was what Marian described as a Gala Lunch – which evidently lived up to its title. At most business lunches the really important question, so it is said, comes up over coffee; but on this occasion it happened a little earlier, when Mr. Paxton said, 'Now, Dr. Wenzel, which will you take – the trifle or the biscuit?'

To which she answered, 'I'll take the biscuit – of course.'

Of course; what else could she possibly have said?

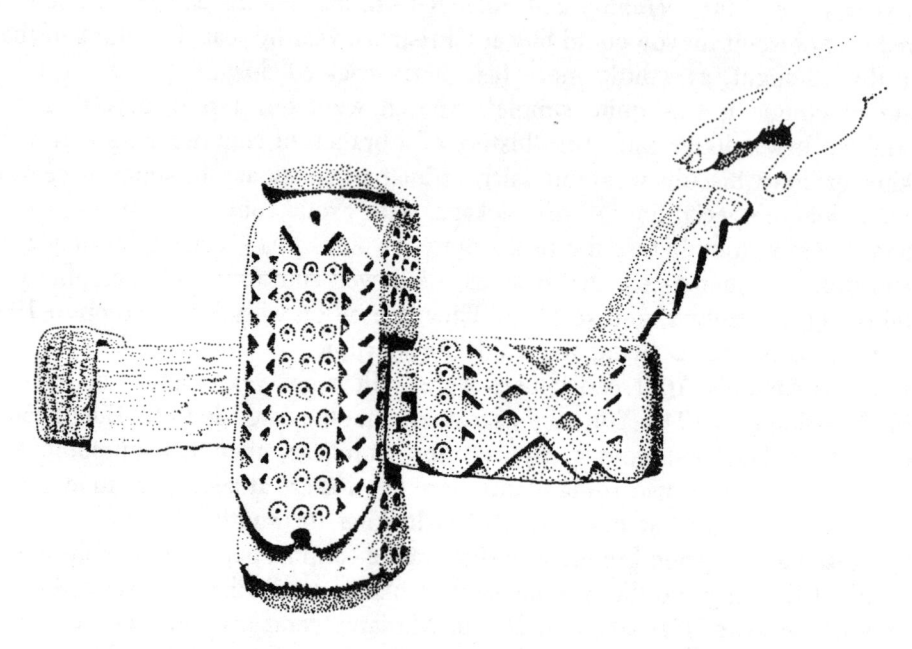

*Nubian wooden lock and key, with carvings to match wall enrichment motifs*

## 18 Place of Birth: Heathrow

This time we were coming home for good. As our plane lost height approaching the airport, Margaret's thoughts took a familiar tack.

'I wonder if the immigration people will say anything this time about my passport? I mean – about where I was born and grew up?'

It never failed to surprise her that in all the years we had been travelling to and from Africa, the control officers at Heathrow had never raised an eyebrow as they stamped her passport. Yet, as she had often remarked, 'I'll bet I'm the only person using this beastly airport that was actually born right here. Right underneath the control tower!'

Which was not strictly true. For when she was born there was no control tower, no airport – just the ancient farmhouse that was her home, lying at the core of its surrounding orchards and fields.

\* \* \* \* \*

180                    *Everything is Possible*

```
                    0      1      2      3      4      5
            inches  ├──────┼──────┼──────┼──────┼──────┤
                    0            5            10           15
        centimetres ├──┬──┬──┬──┬──┬──┬──┬──┬──┬──┬──┬──┬──┬──┬──┤
```

On fine days (and when Margaret was a child the sun was usually shining!) she liked best playing around the pond, where there were sticklebacks galore, roach, redthroats and jack. In a boat made from half a wooden barrel, she made regular voyages to the woody island which rose from the centre of the pond. Blotto, her liver coloured Irish water spaniel needed no assistance from the tub-ferry for she was, of course, by nature a born swimmer – which was convenient, since she too liked the island.

Dominating the island was a majestic full-grown weeping willow. In summer its long, thin, bright green leaves were draped in profusion from every one of its orangey-brown stems. There, beneath that tree, within the enclosure of its fronded veil, was Margaret's most secret place of all.

Wet days were good as well. In the beamed attic of Perry Oaks Farm Margaret had a world of her own into which grown-ups did not intrude. Sometimes she might play with mice which she released from the cages in which they had been caught on the farm. But her favourite occupation was to harness her lovely painted lead cart-horses to ploughs, rollers or hay-rakes which they drew laboriously over make-believe fields. Surrounding these cast-lead figures with others from her collection, she created a rustic vision which, represented symbolically on the attic's long trestle table, lived complete in her imagination.

*Pottery: Neolithic bowl c. 2300 BC. From Heathrow, now in Museum of London*

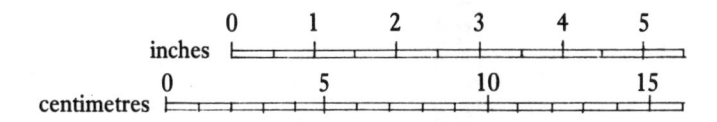

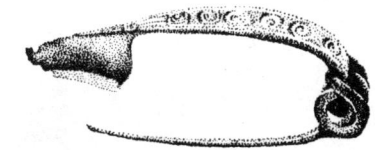

*Bronze brooch, 1st century AD. From Heathrow, now in Museum of London. Actual size.*

On to the screen of Margaret's mind, in the dim vastness of the attic, the outside world projected its image as in a *camera obscura*: the old farmhouse, hemmed in by equally ancient barns and stables, and the farm itself, buzzing with every sort of activity, couched amid the rich, flat acres that the Whittingtons had farmed for more than three hundred years. History was in their name: their ancestor, Sir Richard, was in his lifetime Lord Mayor of London and in the ensuing centuries a folk hero immortalised in pantomime as Dick Whittington. But history was even more deeply embedded in their land: the Whittingtons were only the latest chapter in an age-old story of farming on that site. Scores of flint tools, bronze artefacts and pottery picked up by Margaret's father from his fields bore witness to cultivations going back to prehistoric times.

When Margaret was very young, most of the land was given over to orchards – Morello cherries (with a few sweet cherries), apples and plums. Between the rows of cherry trees Margaret's father grew gillyflowers which he sent to market with the ripe fruit. It was fun to climb the sweet cherry trees to feast on the fruit. Blotto liked sweet cherries, too; but not being a climber, she had to wait expectantly below, catching the fruit as it dropped to her and spitting out the stones from the corner of her mouth.

Most weekdays, long before dawn, some of the great shire horses were harnessed to the firm's massive canary-yellow carts to take the loads of fruit and flowers to the Whittingtons' stall in Covent Garden. Margaret delighted in the colours and craftsmanship of the carts – the vivid background enlivened by hand-lined decoration of black and red picking out the individual structural members of the body, wheel rims and shafts; and the black harness lovingly polished and enriched with gleaming brass accoutrements.

There were only two public roads anywhere near the farm and even these were 'dirt' roads on which any summer traffic created clouds of dust, filming the gleaming

*Place of Birth: Heathrow* 183

bodywork of the black, vermilion-lined pony trap, with its elegantly curved shafts and burnished wheel hubs, which Margaret loved to drive.

One of the dirt roads led to the Bath Road, nowadays referred to as the A4; and although this road is now virtually paralleled by the M4 motorway, it is still very busy. It was different when Margaret was young. From the age of seven, her journeys to school by pony and trap always included a short stretch of the Bath Road, but even when she was of age to drive the whole way herself – in company with an elder – the traffic on the Bath Road was never a worrying problem. Away in the Midlands Mr. Morris had become Sir William and was well on the way to being Lord Nuffield; and an ever-increasing stream of cars was beginning to flow from the factories; but still in sequestered places the old horse-going ways lived on, doomed but not yet ready to die.

By the time we were married in Harmondsworth parish church, not long before war broke out in 1939, the triumph of the internal combustion engine was obvious to everyone. Yet few of us guessed quite how far-reaching the effects of this revolution would be – how it would utterly transform the centuries-old, apparently immutable peace of even such places as Perry Oaks Farm.

Soon after the war began, Pa Whittington left the farm to settle near Cambridge, where he recommenced his farming career; and Perry Oaks Farm passed into the hands of Margaret's Uncle Arthur and Aunt Jessie. Neither of us went back to the Heathrow area until we flew to Khartoum in August 1957. By that time the Tudor farmhouse had long since disappeared, and the orchards and meadows were well on the way to being covered with hangars and runways.

Long before this, of course, Margaret had always been on the alert to see what the newspapers had to say about the new airport. The London *Evening Standard*, for instance, had published a 'story', well illustrated with photos, which might have brought tears to Margaret's eyes if she had been the crying sort. There was the house itself; 'Farmer Whittington' (as the newspaper had called him); his dog Peggy; Mrs. Whittington in her kitchen – and in the background the Radiation gas cooker which Margaret had bought for her father during the time when she had been a cookery demonstrator for the manufacturers.

A banner headline, THREE ACRES OF HISTORY WHERE BUSIEST AIRPORT IS PLANNED, spanned the article; but the text underneath it by the *Standard's* reporter, Arthur La Bern, made it clear that the government intended to take not merely the three acres on which the farm and its gardens stood, but all the land belonging to it as well. 'Farmer Whittington' appeared in the character of John Bull, defending his right to stay put and stoutly claming 'Perry Oaks is far too historic to pull down'. Enlarging on this theme, he told Mr. La Bern how the last wolf in England had been shot there, and how King Edward the Seventh had lunched in the front room of the farmhouse when out hunting from Windsor (a story which, when it was told to her, conjured up in Margaret's childish mind a vision of mountains of duckling and icecream washed down with Niagaras of fizzy lemonade). But Aunt Jessie showed more realism: she admitted to a presentiment that one day they'd have a 'bulldozer coming up the garden'; and as the interview drew to its close even Uncle Arthur allowed himself not merely to contemplate the unthinkable, but to sound a trifle philosophical about it: 'Well, I suppose when this airport does come – IF it does come – it will make things a bit livleier here. It's rather lonely at times here ... no-one to talk to.'

The bulldozer did come – not one, but many; and not only bulldozers, but even more massive earth-moving machines. Within twelve months of the publication of the interview, Perry Oaks Farm had vanished.

But it had not gone completely. The splendid timber construction of its great barn was carefully dismantled, each member being numbered and shipped to the USA where it was re-erected. Many of its bricks were saved for re-use in repair work at Hampton Court. Farmhouse and Palace were of the same age, and it seems quite possible that bricks for both were made in a kiln near Perry Oaks Pond – a supposition borne out by the ancient once-molten bricks, of a kind used in old kilns, which were found in the bank walls of the pond.

\* \* \* \* \*

Now touchdown was very close. We had a fleeting glimpse of Heathrow and concrete strips; wide roads on which cars and lorries were speeding back and forth; a vast jumble of sheds and the impedimenta of an industrialised society. Not a trace of the Heathrow of Margaret's childhood remained, save the tower of Harmondsworth church tucked away behind the Penguin Books factory.

Here we were, in the last days of the dying year, and at the end of my eight years' employment by the Sudanese Republic, being greeted at the airport by Geoffrey Hutton, one of our former Hull students. Margaret was tucking her passport in her rucksack, muttering the customary observation – had it developed into a complaint? – that the Immigration Officer hadn't noticed her place of birth. Soon Geoffrey was driving us slowly down Oxford Street and Regent Street into Piccadilly Circus, so that we could see the illuminations. It was Christmas Eve; thousands of people were milling about in a frenzy of last-minute gift buying.

We were happy. At that moment, if we had given a thought to the Sudan, it would have seemed a million miles away. Only later did we realise how close it was going to be to us for the rest of our days.

*Our Sudanese cats: mother and daughter here seen sharing a kitten*

# *Acknowledgements*

To thank adequately the many who have helped in the preparation of this book is impossible. Those who figure in its pages, such as Margaret Shinnie, Marian Wenzel, Abdel Basit, Halim Awad and Hassan Atabani, have contributed much that can be deduced from the text and much more than cannot. On specific points a host of organizations and individuals have responded to our requests for advice or verification: these include Associated Biscuits Ltd. (Michael Paxton), The London Fire Brigade Service (Jim O'Sullivan), the Gordon Boys School (Headmaster, Michael Kirk), The Company of Veteran Motorists (A.O. Ledger), The Museum of London (Jean Macdonald), Brigadier J.H.S. Lacey of the Royal Engineers, Peter Wolf (Leiter des Deutschen Kulturinstituis, Khartoum) and The Sudan Ministry of Information (for permission to make drawings from two photographs) – to mention only a few of the many.

The problem of singling out individuals is even more acute in regard to the Sudan itself. We would have liked to name the numerous architects who in 1978 took time off from their busy practices to make our 'return' visit so memorable and fruitful. Instead we must confine ourselves to mentioning only two: Elamin Muddathir (that same Elamin whom we found burning the midnight oil at the most crucial moment of the Examination Hall project), who conceived and arranged the visit; and Abden Halim Awad, who provided lavish hospitality and did us many other kindnesses at that time.

Above all our thanks are due to Noel Carrington, who first urged us to write the book and persistently encouraged us over a period of years; and to Kenneth Pinnock, who shaped our first drafts into publishable form. Our book owes its existence very largely indeed to the pertinacity of these two old friends.

Writing this book has indeed taught us that with old friends at hand, 'everything is possible' – even some things that at first seemed difficult or impossible. In the final stages of its preparation, the willingness of our friends to help at every turn has continuied to show itself – almost, at times, to the point of embarrassment. The Index we owe to the kindness of Arthur Spencer; and we find ourselves (thanks no doubt to our own inefficiency) provided with no fewer than three calligraphic versions of the title, all different and each delightful. Two of these by the same hand, appear on the jacket and the title page, and are acknowledged separately. The third, by Mohamed Alamin Ali of Khartoum, forms an appropriate and beautiful tailpiece to these acknowledgements.

## Some Books on the Sudan

Adams, W.Y., *Nubia: Corridor to Africa* (London 1977).
Beshir, Mohammed Said, *The Sudan: Crossroads of Africa* (London 1965).
Greenlaw, Jean-Pierre. *The Coral Buildings of Suakin (London 1976)*.
Holt, P.M., *A Modern History of the Sudan* (London 1961).
Magnus, Philip, *Kitchener – Portrait of an Imperialist* (London 1958).
Moorehead, Alan, *The White Nile* (London 1960).
Moorehead, Alan, *The Blue Nile* (London 1962).
Sandes, Lieut. Colonel E.W.C. *The Royal Engineers in Egypt and the Sudan* (Chatham 1937).
Sartorius, Ernestine, *The Soudan Three Months in the Soudan* (London 1885).
Shinnie, Margaret, *Ancient African Kingdoms* (London 1965).
Shinnie, P.L. *Merce: A civilisation of the Sudan* (London 1967).
Wenzel, Marian, *House Decoration in Nubia* (London 1972).

# Index

Abdalla el Radi, 157
Abdel Basit, 111ff., 122, 123, 124, 147, 156
Abdullahi Hassan, 136
Aberarth, 97
Aberystwyth, 94ff., 139
Abu Simbel, 104, 171
Acropolis, 79
Adam Ibrahim el Hag, 32
Adam Mohammed Bushara, 132
Agriculture, Minister of, 46
Akasha, 74
Alberti, Leon Battista, 43
Allah el Tayar, Sheikh, 122, 124
Alexandria, 104
Amada, Temple of, 104
*angareeb* (bed), 153
El Amin Muddathir, 51
Archaeology, Commissioner for, 105
Architectural Association, 23
Architecture, School of, or Department of, 13, 31, 33, 83
Arrol Johnston motor car, 92
Aswan High Dam, 76, 118
el Atabani, Ahmed, 20
el Atabani, Galal, 20
el Atabani, Hassan Mohammed, 17ff., 45
el Atabani, Ibrahim Rushdi, 20
el Atabani, Mohammed, Brigadier, 19, 25
Atbara, 138, 139
Athens, 79
el Azhari, Ismail, 105

banian tree, 54, 55, 56, 85
bas-reliefs, 76, 83, 84
Batahin, 68
battles; of Messellemiya Gate, 19, 25; of Omdurmam, 87, 102, 131, 178
beads, 18
Belfast, 122
Bennett College, 22
Berlin Museum, 76
Bernard Boda Gette, 32, 34
Birmingham, 68
Blaenau Ffestiniog, 124
Blue Nile River, 29, 86, 108, 165; Bridge, 73, 104, 105, 142
B.O.A.C., 68
Bolis Salib, 81
Bridgeman, Mr. (architect), 20
British Ambassador, 81
British Council, 111, 114
British Embassy, 24
British Library, 177
'The Building News', 30
Burckhardt, 171
Burri, 55
Bursa, 40, 42, 50

Cairo, 78
calligraphy, Islamic, 42, 50ff.
cap (*taqia*), 139, 145
Cathedral, Coventry, 24; St. David's, 144
cats, 56, 148, 150, 172
S.S. Cedardine, 104

Chapman-Andrews, Sir Edwin, 108
Chatham, School of Military Engineering, 102, 109, 110
churches, 83, 133, 138
Churchill, Sir Winston, 131
cinema-screens, 93, 94
Colleges, Bennett, 22; Gordon Memorial, 7, 20, 31, 40, 44, 58, 70
Cologne, Radio Symphony Orchestra of, 65, 70
Committee, University Building, 44ff.
Condominium, Anglo-Egyptian, 7, 31, 87, 148
Covent Garden, 182
Crewe, 68
Cromer, Lord, 40
cycling, 86

Daoud (messenger), 112, 130, 136, 138, 158, 161
ed Debba, 133
Debeira (West), 118, 120
decoration of houses in Nubia, 170ff.
Departments; of Architecture, Khartoum University, 13, 31, 33, 83; of forestry, 48, 63; of Public Works, 20
Derby, 20
Disougi el Amin (driver), 131, 132, 137
dizziness, 76ff.
Dongola el Aguz, 133
Ed Dueim, 31

education, 31
Edwards, Amelia, 76
El Amin (Elamin) Muddathir, 51, 81
'El Sudan El Gadid', 108
Enthoven, Roddy, 24
'The Evening Standard', 184
Examination Hall, 39ff., 53ff., 61ff.
Ezzat Kasser, 90ff.

Fabricius Bey, 31
Faras, 82
Farmer & Dark, Messrs., 112
Finance, Minister of, 108
fire engines, 94
fisherman, 154ff.
Ford, E. Onslow, R.A., 102
Forestry, Department of, 48, 63
Francis, G.E., 20, 22
frescoes, 82

*Ful Sudani* (peanuts), 25, 26

Gabir Abdul Izz, 53, 54, 55, 61, 67, 70
*gellabiya* (mens' robe), 162
Georgian Society, The, 13
Gereif, 31
El Geyf, 147
Ghana, University of, 118
Gharieb Allah, Sheikh, 122, 123, 125, 127
el Ghazali, 138
Gobara, Ahmed el Mahdi, 45, 46, 54, 55, 57, 58, 60, 93ff.
Goethe Institut, 65
Gordon Boys' School, 109
Gordon, General Charles, 19, 20, 101, 102, 147
Gordon Memorial College, 7, 20, 31, 40, 44, 58, 70
Gorringe, Lieutenant, R.E., 29ff.
Graham, Ann, 130, 139, 143
'The Graphic', 151
*gubbas* (graves), 19, 123, 124, 125, 133
*guffa* (flexible basket), 18, 25, 26

el Hadi Yousif Ali, 144, 145
el Hag, Adam Ibrahim, 32
Hagia Sophia, 65
Halim Awad, 83, 124ff.
Hampton Court, 184, 185
Harmondsworth, 183
Hassan Araby, 174ff.
Hassan el Bahar, 163ff.
Hassan Daffala, 74
Hassan Yassin Bedawi, 131, 132, 142
Hatshepsut, Queen, 76
Heathrow, 13, 179
Horticultural Hall, 23
houses; Khalifa's 87, 88; in Nubia, 170ff., 17, Sharia el Gamhuria, 21, 22, 24, 25, 90, 167
*howareen* (followers), 123, 126
Hull, 12, 13
Huntley and Palmers, 177, 178
*huq* (spice burner), 163ff.
Hutton, Geoffrey, 185

Ibrahim (Sayed Ibrahim) Ahmed, 35ff.
*imma* (turban), 139
insects, 133ff.
Insinger, Jan, 76
'Investigation of Buildings in Wadi Halfa and

## Index

Adjoining Villages', 170
Istanbul, 40, 41

Jebel Barkal, 137, 138
Jebel Merkhiyat, 131
Jiddah, 148
Juba, 46, 48, 63

Khalifa's House, 87, 88
Khartoum, 8, 14; market, 27ff.; University, *see* University
King George V, 22
Kitchener, Field-Marshall the Lord, 29, 74, 87, 101, 102, 104, 105, 108, 109, 110
Kumma, 75

Le Bern, Arthur, 184
Lepsius, 76
S.S. Lesbian, 104
Liverpool, 14
Levin, Ezra, 9, 44ff.
London, 80, 111ff.
Luton, 143
Luxor, 78

Mahdi's Tomb, 87
*mahfeeza* (purse), 139
maps, 129ff.
March, Sydney, 104, 105
Mekki Shibeika, 167
*mercub* (slippers), 55, 165
Merowe, 138
Merowe, Ancient, 140
Messellemiya Gate, Battle of, 19, 25
*mimaryeen* (architects), 33, 34
Milton, John, 85, 86
Minister; of Agriculture, 46; of Finance, 108; of Public Building and Works, 17, 45; of Supply, 94; of Transport, 46
Misrair, 68
model of Examination Hall, 48ff.
Mogran Point, 86, 87
Mohammed Mamoud Hamdi, 132, 138, 143
monastry (of el Ghazali), 138
mosques, 42, 124, 125, 144
motor-cars, 87, 89ff.
Muhafaza, the, 148, 150
*muhendis* (engineer, pl. *muhendiseen*), 28, 31, 32, 34

museums; Berlin, 76; Mahdia, 87, 88, 92; Merowe, 136; National, 81; (old) Sudan, 109, 159; Zoological, 163
*murasla* (messenger), 112
Muttalib Balla Ahmed, 31

Napata, 136, 138
Naqa, 140
el Nasser, Gamal Abd., President, 53
*neem* trees, 85
Nile, River, 7, 36, 68, 75, 78, 104, 117, 133, 139, 140
el Nilein Mosque, 144
Nimeiri, President, 9
Nubia, 35ff., 74, 83, 104, 136, 159, 161; house decoration in, 170ff.
Nuri, 139, 143
Nyala, 32

old woman in black, 61, 71
Omdurman, 8, 14, 68, 87, 106, 108, 122, 124, 148; Battle of, 87, 102, 131, 178; shops in, 17
Omer Agra, 81
Osman Digna, 151
Osman Waqialla, 66, 67

Palace, Governor-General's 19, 28, 30, 86, 104
Pantheon, 64
'Paradise Lost', 85
Paxton, Mr. 177, 178
peanuts (*Ful Sudani*), 25, 26
Perry Oaks Farm, 180, 184
Port Sudan, 22, 68, 105, 147, 148, 154
Primrose Hill, 181
Public Works, Department of, 20; Ministry of, 17, 45
purse (*mahfeeza*), 139
pyramids, 136, 137, 139, 140, 143

Queen Mary, 22
Queen's University of Belfast, 122

Red Sea, 105, 147, 148, 154
Reicha, Herr Wilhelm, 70
'The River War', 131
Robertson, Howard, 23
Royal Academy, 102
Royal Engineers, 29ff.
Royal Institute of British Architects, 23

St Andrew's University, 94
St David's Cathedral, 144
Salamat el Basha, 73
Sartorious, General, 151
Sartorious, Mrs. and Miss, 152, 153
scarlet fever, 65
Schools, Engineering High, 31; Gordon Boys', 109; of Military Engineering, 102, 109; Wadi Seidna, 20, 21
Semna East, 74, 75, 76, 83, 84, 171
Senusret III, 76, 83
Shambat, 73
Sharia el Gamhuria 17 (Potters' house), 21, 22, 24, 25, 90, 167
Sheffield, 68
'shell' method of building, 44ff.
Shellal, 78, 104
Shendi, 138, 140
Shiner, George, 170
Shinnie, Margaret, 9, 117, 122
Shinnie, Professor Peter, 118, 122
shop-signs, 27ff.
slippers (*merkub*), 55, 57, 165
Spence, Sir Basil, 23, 24
spice-burner (*huq*), 163ff.
Spragg, Bill, 23
Stamitz, Carl, 70
statues, 101ff.
Students' Union building, 163
Suakin, 147ff.
Sudan Museum, 109, 159
'Sudan Notes and Records', 151
*Sudd*, 63
*sunt* forest, 85, 92
Supply, Ministry of, 94

*taqia* (cap), 139, 145
temperature, 65, 85
temples, 76, 104, 140
Thabit Hassan Thabit, 105
timber, provision of, 46, 63
Timber Research and Development Association, 44

'The Times', 55, 81, 106, 107, 109, 110
*tobe* (ladies dress), 142, 162
trains, 7, 73, 74, 161, 162
Transport, Minister of, 46
trees, 85, 86
Uli Cami Mosque (Bursa), 42, 44, 50
U.N.E.S.C.O., 118
University; of St. Andrew's 94; of Belfast, 122; of Ghana, 118; of Khartoum, 7, 8, 9, 13, 31; Appointment Boards, 94; Department of Architecture, 13, 31, 33, 83; Examination Hall, 39ff., 53ff., 61ff.; Faculty of Engineering 32; Faculty of Law, 54; Pro-Vice-Chancellor, 167; Registrar, *see* Gobara; Resident Engineer, 163ff.; Students' Union Building, 163; Vice-Chancellor, 47, 51, 57ff.

Varian's shop, 88
Vice Chancellor of Khartoum University, 47, 51, 57ff.

Wadi Halfa, 7, 35, 73, 74, 76, 78, 117, 170
Wadi Maqaddam, 131
Wadi Seidna, 20, 21
Wake, Richard, 151
*wali* (magician), 154-6
Wau, 32, 34, 94
Wenzel, Dr. Marian, 122, 169ff.
White Nile, River, 19, 46, 62, 86; Bridge, 83, 87
Whittington, Sir Richard ('Dick Whittington'), 181
the 'whoosh', 121ff.
Wingate, Sir Francis Reginald, 87, 104, 108
Woking, 109

*zeer* (waterpot), 119, 120
*zikr* (ritual dance), 123, 124, 126
Zoological Museum, 163
Zuma, 137

Arthur Spencer
British Embassy, Khartoum
1959–1961